DENMARK VESEY'S BIBLE

DENMARK VESEY'S BIBLE

THE THWARTED REVOLT THAT PUT
SLAVERY AND SCRIPTURE ON TRIAL

JEREMY SCHIPPER

PRINCETON UNIVERSITY PRESS

PRINCETON AND OXFORD

Published by Princeton University Press
41 William Street, Princeton, New Jersey 08540
99 Banbury Road, Oxford OX2 6JX

press.princeton.edu

All Rights Reserved
First paperback printing, 2024
Paperback ISBN 9780691259314

The Library of Congress has cataloged the cloth edition as follows:

Names: Schipper, Jeremy, author.
Title: Denmark Vesey's Bible : the thwarted revolt that put slavery and scripture on trial / Jeremy Schipper.
Description: Princeton : Princeton University Press, 2022. | Includes bibliographical references and index.
Identifiers: LCCN 2021016614 (print) | LCCN 2021016615 (ebook) | ISBN 9780691192864 (hardback) | ISBN 9780691212678 (ebook)
Subjects: LCSH: Vesey, Denmark, approximately 1767–1822—Trials, litigation, etc. | Bible—Black interpretations. | Slave insurrections—South Carolina—Charleston—History. | Slavery and the church. | Charleston (S.C.)—History—Slave Insurrection, 1822.
Classification: LCC F279.C49 N478 2022 (print) | LCC F279.C49 (ebook) | DDC 975.7/91503092—dc23
LC record available at https://lccn.loc.gov/2021016614
LC ebook record available at https://lccn.loc.gov/2021016615

British Library Cataloging-in-Publication Data is available

Editorial: Fred Appel and James Collier
Production Editorial: Sara Lerner
Text Design: Karl Spurzem
Jacket/Cover Design: Emily Weigel
Production: Erin Suydam
Publicity: Kate Hensley and Kathryn Stevens
Copyeditor: Beth Gianfagna

Jacket/Cover Credit: Adaptation of *Vesey Talking to His People* by Dorothy B. Wright. Photo: Rick Rhodes Photography. Courtesy of the City of Charleston, South Carolina

This book has been composed in Arno Pro with Irby display

To my brothers, Timothy and James Schipper

Remember Denmark Vesey of Charleston.

—FREDERICK DOUGLASS, ROCHESTER,
NEW YORK, MARCH 2, 1863

CONTENTS

LIST OF ILLUSTRATIONS

LIST OF MAJOR FIGURES

Mary Lamboll Beach (1770–1851): A local slaveholding widow who, in the summer of 1822, wrote her sister Elizabeth L. Gilchrist several letters with details about the events surrounding Vesey's plot (see chapters 1, 2, 3, 4, and 5).

Batteau Bennett (d. 1822): Enslaved by South Carolina Governor Thomas Bennett Jr., Batteau was one of the five alleged ringleaders executed alongside Vesey on July 2, 1822 (see chapter 2).

Ned Bennett (d. 1822): Enslaved by South Carolina Governor Thomas Bennett Jr., Ned was one of the five alleged ringleaders of the plot. Along with Joe La Roche, Ned was said to have attempted to recruit George Wilson to join Vesey's plot. Ned was executed alongside Vesey on July 2, 1822 (see the introduction and chapter 2).

Rolla Bennett (d. 1822): Enslaved by South Carolina Governor Thomas Bennett Jr., Rolla was one of the five alleged ringleaders executed alongside Vesey on July 2, 1822. Along with Jesse Blackwood, he was one of the two alleged ringleaders to confess about the planning of Vesey's plot, including Vesey's use of biblical texts (see chapters 1 and 2).

Thomas Bennett Jr. (1781–1865): The governor of South Carolina during the trial and execution of Vesey and his associates. He enslaved three of the accused ringleaders (Batteau, Ned, and Rolla). John L. Wilson succeeded him as governor later in 1822.

Jesse Blackwood (d. 1822): Enslaved by a local bank president named Thomas Blackwood, Jesse was one of the five alleged ringleaders executed alongside Vesey on July 2, 1822. Along with Rolla Bennet, he was one of the two alleged ringleaders to confess about the planning of Vesey's plot, including Vesey's use of biblical texts (see chapters 1 and 2).

Artemas Boies (1792–1844): A minister at the Second Presbyterian Church, which admitted Vesey into the congregation's communion on April 12, 1817. Along with Benjamin Parker and Richard Furman, he was said to have visited Vesey and the other accused ringleaders in jail shortly before they were hanged (see chapter 4).

Morris Brown (1770–1849): Helped to found two independent African Methodist churches in 1818. In August 1822, he was convicted of violating a South Carolina law prohibiting free persons of African descent from leaving and then returning to the state. He was given fifteen days to leave the state. Brown fled to Philadelphia, where he would eventually succeed Richard Allen, becoming the second bishop of the African Methodist Episcopal Church (see the introduction).

Arthur Buist (1799–1843): A minister at the First Presbyterian Church. On November 7, 1822, he preached "On the Doctrine of Particular Providence," a sermon that interprets the suppression of Vesey's plot as an example of God's active and continued involvement in the world (see chapter 5).

George W. Cross (1783–1836): Denmark Vesey's former landlord, who served as Vesey's defense attorney at his trial. In 1823, he joined the South Carolina Association, a vigilance organization formed in the wake of the Vesey plot, owing to concerns that laws intended to control people of African descent in Charleston were not rigorously enforced.

Yorrick Cross (lifespan unknown): Enslaved by Vesey's attorney, George W. Cross, Yorrick testified about the planning of Vesey's plot.

Frederick Dalcho (1770–1836): Born in London, Dalcho studied medicine in Baltimore before settling in Charleston in 1799. Eventually, he studied theology and became an Episcopal priest, serving at Saint Michael's Church in Charleston until his death. Writing under the pseudonym "a South Carolinian," he published a thirty-eight-page proslavery pamphlet titled *Practical Considerations Founded on the Scriptures, Relative to the Slave Population of South-Carolina.* The pamphlet makes a case that while the Bible does not prohibit slavery, it requires religious instruction for everyone, including enslaved persons (see chapter 6).

Henry Drayton (d. 1837): Helped found two independent African Methodist churches with Morris Brown in 1818. Along with Morris Brown, he was convicted in August 1822 of violating a South Carolina law prohibiting free persons of African descent from leaving and then returning to the state. He was given fifteen days to leave the state (see the introduction).

Benjamin Elliott (1786–1836): A native of Charleston who trained as a lawyer in Princeton, New Jersey, at an institution then known as the College of New Jersey (later renamed Princeton University). Writing under the pseudonym "A South Carolinian," Elliott published a proslavery article about Vesey's plot titled "To Our Northern Brethren" in the local newspaper *City Gazette and Commercial Daily Advertiser.* Elliott's article includes several key biblical texts, not mentioned in the published trial transcripts, that Vesey and his associates allegedly used to promote the plot (see chapter 1).

John Enslow (d. 1822): Enslaved by a merchant named Joseph Enslow, John testified regarding Vesey's use of Exodus 21:16 among other biblical texts. Charleston's mayor, James Hamilton Jr., described the evidence John provided as "much appreciated by the Court." John died while imprisoned in the workhouse awaiting his banishment (see the introduction and chapter 1).

Richard Furman (1755–1825): A Baptist minister said to have visited Vesey and the other accused ringleaders in jail shortly before their executions. He wrote an influential pamphlet titled *Rev. Dr. Furman's Exposition of the Views of the Baptists Relative to the Coloured Population of the United States, in a Communication to the Governor of South-Carolina*. Over the next several decades, Furman's pamphlet would shape paternalistic ideas about slavery in the antebellum imagination (see chapter 5).

Monday Gell (lifespan unknown): Enslaved by a stable owner named John Gell, Monday was a skilled harness maker who provided the court with the names of forty-two other conspirators after Vesey and the five other accused ringleaders were executed. The court reduced Monday's death sentence to banishment in light of the information he provided in his confessions (see the introduction).

Jacob Glen (d. 1822): Enslaved by John S. Glen, Jacob, also known as Jack, was said to have interpreted the Bible during meetings at which the conspiracy was planned. He was one of the twenty-two men executed on July 26, 1822, for allegedly participating in Vesey's plot. Charleston's mayor, James Hamilton Jr., identified Jacob as a preacher (see the introduction).

Daniel Hall (lifespan unknown): A local Methodist minister who was said to have visited Vesey and his associates in jail. According to court records, he heard the confessions of Rolla Bennett and Jesse Blackwood shortly before their executions on July 2, 1822 (see chapter 1).

James Hamilton Jr. (1786–1857): Intendent, or mayor, of Charleston in 1822. Later, he would serve as a member of the United States House of Representatives and as the governor of South Carolina. On June 19, 1822, Hamilton organized a Court of Magistrates and Freeholders, with Lionel Henry Kennedy and Thomas Parker serving as magistrates. The court would conduct the trials of Vesey and others accused of involvement in the conspiracy. In mid-August, Hamilton published some of the court documents as a forty-six-page pamphlet titled *An Account of the Late Intended Insurrection among a Portion of the Blacks of the City* (see the introduction and chapter 2).

Bacchus Hammet (d. 1822): Enslaved by a merchant named Benjamin Hammet, Bacchus testified regarding Vesey's use of Exodus 21:16 among other biblical texts. He was one of the twenty-two men hanged on July 26, 1822, for allegedly participating in Vesey's plot (see the introduction and chapter 1).

Mingo Harth (d. 1822): Enslaved by a lumber merchant named William Harth, Mingo was implicated by William Paul and arrested on May 31, 1822. According to William Paul's testimony, some of the planning meetings for Vesey's plot were held at Mingo's house. Mingo was one of the twenty-two men executed on July 26, 1822, for allegedly participating in Vesey's plot (see the introduction).

Lionel Henry Kennedy (1787?–1847): A Yale-educated lawyer who, along with Thomas Parker, served as a magistrate for the Court of Magistrates and Freeholders that tried Vesey and the others accused of involvement in Vesey's plot. With Parker, he edited *An Official Report of the Trials of Sundry Negroes, Charged with an Attempt to Raise an Insurrection in the State of South-Carolina* (see chapter 3). Kennedy and Parker also prepared trial transcripts for the South Carolina House of Representatives, docketed as "Document B House of Representatives," and a longer version for the South Carolina Senate, docketed as "Evidence Document B." Consult the appendix for a transcript of Kennedy's sentence of Denmark Vesey; Jack Pritchard, also known as "Gullah Jack"; and ten other enslaved persons sentenced collectively.

Joe La Roche (lifespan unknown): Enslaved by Mary La Roche, Joe La Roche, along with Ned Bennett, allegedly attempted to recruit George Wilson to join Vesey's plot. At the trial of Rolla Bennett, Joe offered detailed testimony about the planning of Vesey's plot (see the introduction).

Benjamin Morgan Palmer (1781–1847): A Congregationalist minister said to have visited Vesey and the other accused ringleaders in jail shortly before they were hanged. He preached "Religion Profitable: With a Special Reference to the Case of Servants," a proslavery sermon that addresses Vesey's plot with a dense network of biblical references (see chapter 4).

Thomas Parker (1793?–1844): A lawyer who, along with Lionel Kennedy, served as a magistrate for the Court of Magistrates and Freeholders that tried Vesey and others accused of involvement in Vesey's plot. With Kennedy, he edited *An Official Report of the Trials of Sundry Negroes, Charged with an Attempt to Raise an Insurrection in the State of South-Carolina.* Kennedy and Parker also prepared trial transcripts for the South Carolina House of Representatives, docketed as "Document B House of Representatives," and a longer version for the South Carolina Senate, docketed as "Evidence Document B" (see chapter 3).

William Paul (lifespan unknown): Enslaved by John Paul, William testified at Vesey's trial that Vesey studied the Bible extensively. Under integration, William implicated Mingo Harth and Paul Poyas. Instead of sentencing him to death, the court banished William (see the introduction).

Peter Poyas (d. 1822): Enslaved by James Poyas, Peter was one of the five alleged ringleaders executed alongside Vesey on July 2, 1822 (see chapter 2).

Peter Prioleau (lifespan unknown): A mixed-race cook who was enslaved by Colonel John Cordes Prioleau, Peter told his slaveholder about Vesey's plot after William Paul attempted to recruit him. William Paul was subsequently interrogated and eventually implicated others. Along with George Wilson, Peter is often remembered as one of the betrayers of Vesey's plot (see the introduction).

Jack Pritchard or "Gullah Jack" (d. 1822): Enslaved by Paul Pritchard, he was known as Gullah Jack or sometimes Couter Jack. He was believed to be one of Vesey's closest coconspirators. According to court documents, which describe Jack as a "sorcerer" and a "doctor," he used traditional African medical and religious practices and was thought to be invincible by some involved in the plot. Lionel Kennedy sentenced him to death on July 9, 1822 (consult the appendix for a transcript of the sentence). Jack was executed on July 12, 1822 (see chapter 3).

Jack Purcell (d. 1822): Enslaved by Ann Smith Bonsell Purcell, Jack allegedly confessed that Vesey used biblical texts to recruit him to join the insurrection plot. He was one of the twenty-two men hanged on July 26, 1822, for allegedly participating in Vesey's plot (see the introduction).

Denmark Vesey (1767?–1822): A formerly enslaved man of African descent who purchased his freedom with his winnings from the East-Bay lottery. He was accused of plotting what could have been the largest insurrection involving enslaved persons in United States history. He was hanged on July 2, 1822 (see the introduction).

Joseph Vesey (1747–1835): Born in Bermuda, Joseph Vesey was a ship captain involved in the slave trade who settled in Charleston. In the early 1780s, he acquired an enslaved young man later known as Denmark Vesey (see the introduction).

George Wilson (lifespan unknown): Enslaved by Major John Wilson, George was a class leader in the African Church. Joe La Roche and Ned Bennett allegedly attempted to recruit him to join Vesey's plot. George told Major Wilson about the plot, and Major Wilson informed James Hamilton, who then informed Governor Bennett. Along with Peter Prioleau, George is often remembered as one of the betrayers of Vesey's plot (see the introduction).

John L. Wilson (1784–1849): Succeeded Thomas Bennett as governor of South Carolina. Wilson endorsed Richard Furman's request for a day of public humiliation and thanksgiving and the publication of Furman's pamphlet as *Rev. Dr. Richard Furman's Exposition of the Views of the Baptists Relative to the Coloured Population of the United States, in a Communication to the Governor of South-Carolina* (see chapter 5).

TIMELINE OF MAJOR EVENTS

Exact dates are provided when available.[1]

1739

September 9. The Stono Rebellion, named for the Stono River about twenty miles southwest of Charleston, is led by an armed group of enslaved Africans. In total, over twenty white people and at least forty Africans were killed (see chapter 2).

1740

South Carolina Assembly passes the Act for the Better Ordering and Governing of Negroes and Other Slaves in This Province, popularly known as the Negro Act of 1740. Article 17 of this act states, "Every Slave who shall raise, or attempt to raise an Insurrection" shall "suffer death" (see chapter 2).

1781

Joseph Vesey transports 390 enslaved persons to Saint-Domingue, including a young man referred to as Telemaque (later known as Denmark Vesey). Telemaque was sold along with the other enslaved men, women, and children in Saint-Domingue (see the introduction).

1782

Joseph Vesey returns to Saint-Domingue. The planter who had purchased Telemaque said that he was "unsound, and subject to epileptic fits." Telemaque is returned to Joseph Vesey, who settles in Charleston (see the introduction).

1799

November 9. Denmark Vesey wins $1,500 in the East-Bay lottery (see the introduction).

December 31. Denmark purchases his freedom for $600. Mary Clodner Vesey, the wife of Joseph Vesey, has papers drawn up that state "from the yoke of Servitude" she has "set free and discharged a certain negro man named Telemaque with all his goods and chattel" (see the introduction).

1805

To supplement the Negro Act of 1740, the South Carolina legislature passes the Act for the Punishment of Certain Crimes against the State of South-Carolina, which rules that not only enslaved persons but "every person or persons" involved in the planning or carrying out of an insurrection would "suffer death." This would include free persons such as Denmark Vesey (see chapter 2).

1817

April 12. Denmark Vesey is admitted to the congregation's communion at the Second Presbyterian Church, although later he is identified as a "class leader" in the African Church (see the introduction and chapter 1).

1818

Morris Brown and Henry Drayton travel to Philadelphia to meet with Richard Allen, a founder and the first bishop of the African Methodist Episcopal Church. Shortly after Brown and Drayton's return to Charleston, two independent African Methodist churches were built in the city (see the introduction).

June 7. The City Guard disrupts services in the African Church and arrests 143 free and enslaved persons of African descent (see the introduction).

1820

The United States Congress reaches what becomes known as the Missouri Compromise. Missouri's request for admission to the Union as a slaveholding state was granted on the condition that Maine be granted admission as a state in which slavery was prohibited. Denmark Vesey mentions the debate surrounding this compromise when recruiting others to his cause (see the introduction).

Twenty-six petitioners identified as "free persons of color, attached to the African Methodist Episcopal Church, in Charleston," including Morris Brown, send a petition in support of their church to the South Carolina House of Representatives. Thirty-two white signatories, including the clergymen Artemas Boies and Benjamin Morgan Palmer, support the petition (see chapter 4).

October 16. A petition with the signatures of over one hundred white persons is sent to the South Carolina legislature. The petition calls for further restrictions on people of African descent. Among other stated concerns, it warns that the African Church in Charleston was supported by "Abolition Societies in the Eastern and Northern States" (see the introduction).

1822

May 25. An enslaved man named William Paul tries to recruit Peter Prioleau, a mixed-race cook who was enslaved by Colonel John Cordes Prioleau, to participate in Vesey's plot. Peter tells his slaveholder about the plot (see the introduction).

May 30. James Hamilton Jr. learns of the plot from John Cordes Prioleau. William Paul is arrested, examined, and placed in solitary confinement (see the introduction).

May 31. William Paul implicates Mingo Harth and Peter Poyas (see the introduction).

June 8. While in solitary confinement, William Paul confesses (see the introduction).

June 9. Joe La Roche and Ned Bennett attempt unsuccessfully to recruit George Wilson, a class leader in the African Church who was enslaved by Major John Wilson (see the introduction).

June 10. Governor Bennett orders the arrests of Mingo Harth, Paul Poyas, and Rolla Bennett (see the introduction).

June 14. George Wilson tells his slaveholder of the plot. Major Wilson informs Hamilton, who then informs Governor Bennett (see the introduction).

June 16. The accused ringleaders are said to have met at Vesey's house. Jack Pritchard, or "Gullah Jack," allegedly tells Yorrick Cross that the revolt will be delayed because the patrols are too strong (see the introduction).

June 19. Hamilton organizes a Court of Magistrates and Freeholders with Lionel Henry Kennedy and Thomas Parker serving as magistrates. William Paul testifies that Vesey "studies all he can to put it into the heads of the blacks to have a rising against the whites" (see the introduction and chapters 1 and 2).

June 22. William Dove, the captain of the City Guard, arrests Vesey. Several witnesses testify before the court (see the introduction).

June 27. The court tries Vesey (see the introduction and chapter 3).

June 28. Kennedy sentences Vesey to death (see the appendix for a transcript of the sentence). Five others accused as "ringleaders" are also sentenced to death: Rolla Bennett, Batteau Bennett, Ned Bennett, Peter Poyas, and Jesse Blackwood (see the introduction and chapter 2).

July 2. Denmark Vesey, along with Batteau Bennett, Ned Bennett, Rolla Bennett, Peter Poyas, and Jesse Blackwood, is hanged (see the introduction and chapter 2).

July 5. Mary Lamboll Beach writes to her sister Elizabeth L. Gilchrist with details about the trials and executions of Vesey and the other accused ringleaders (see chapters 1, 2, 3, 4, and 5).

July 9. Lionel Kennedy sentences Jack Pritchard, commonly known as Gullah Jack, to death (consult the appendix for a transcript of the sentence). Kennedy also sentences ten other enslaved persons—Charles Billings, Jemmy Clement, Jerry Cohen, Bacchus Hammet, Dean Mitchell, William Paul, Adam Robertson, Dick Sims, Bellisle Yates, and Naphur Yates—to death (see the appendix for a transcript of the collective sentence of the ten enslaved persons).

July 12. John Horry and Jack Pritchard are executed. In a confession dated July 12, Bacchus Hammet allegedly stated that at one meeting "a large Book like a Bible was open before them" at Denmark Vesey's house.

July 14. Vesey's first proposed date for the insurrection.

July 26. Twenty-two enslaved persons, including Bacchus Hammet and Jack Purcell, are executed. The first Court of Magistrates and Freeholders adjourns.

August 2. William Garner arrives in Charleston as a prisoner.

August 3. The organization of a second Court of Magistrates and Freeholders is announced. William Garner is convicted and sentenced to death.

August 6. Judge John B. White rules that Morris Brown and Henry Drayton had violated an 1821 South Carolina law prohibiting free persons of African descent from leaving and then returning to the state. He gives them fifteen days to leave the state.

August 9. William Garner is executed, bringing the total to thirty-five persons executed for alleged involvement in Vesey's plot.

Mid-August. Hamilton publishes some of the court documents as a forty-six-page pamphlet titled *An Account of the Late Intended Insurrection among a Portion of the Blacks of the City* (see chapter 2).

September 22. Benjamin Morgan Palmer preaches *Religion Profitable: With a Special Reference to the Case of Servants*, a proslavery sermon that addresses Vesey's plot with a dense network of biblical references (see chapter 4).

September 26. The Charleston Bible Society's board of managers sends a letter to Governor Bennett requesting that he declare a "day of public humiliation and thanksgiving" in recognition of God's deliverance of the city from Vesey's plot. Governor Bennett denies the request (see chapter 5).

October 7. Judge Elihu Hall Bay convicts four men identified as "white" (William Allen, Jacob Danders, John Igneshias, and Andrew S. Rhodes) on the charge of "a Misdemeanor in inciting Slaves to Insurrection." The court notes that there is no solid evidence that these four men were actually involved in Vesey's plot (see the introduction and chapter 2).

Mid-October. Kennedy and Parker publish the 202-page *An Official Report of the Trials of Sundry Negroes, Charged with an Attempt to Raise an Insurrection in the State of South-Carolina.* They also prepare trial transcripts for the South Carolina House of Representatives, docketed as "Document B House of Representatives," and a longer version for the South Carolina Senate, docketed as "Evidence Document B." The transcription of these documents, however, was not completed until November 1822 (see the introduction and chapter 3).

November 7. The Reverend Arthur Buist preaches "On the Doctrine of Particular Providence" at the First Presbyterian Church. The sermon understands the suppression of Vesey's plot as an example of God's active and continued involvement in the world (see chapter 5).

December 24. The Baptist minister Richard Furman writes a nineteen-page letter to the new South Carolina governor, John L. Wilson, once again requesting a day of public humiliation and thanksgiving. The letter is published in 1823 as *Rev. Dr. Richard Furman's Exposition of the Views of the Baptists Relative to the Coloured Population of the United States, in a Communication to the Governor of South-Carolina* (see chapter 5).

1823

Mid-July. Prominent white citizens of Charleston, including the lawyer for Vesey's defense, create a vigilance organization called the "South Carolina Association" in response to concerns that laws intended to control people of African descent in Charleston were not rigorously enforced (see chapter 6).

Late-July. Frederick Dalcho, an Episcopalian minister at Saint Michael's Church in Charleston, writing under the pseudonym "a South Carolinian," publishes a thirty-eight-page proslavery pamphlet titled *Practical Considerations Founded on the Scriptures, Relative to the Slave Population of South-Carolina* (see chapter 6).

PREFACE

In June 1822, an obscure lawyer from Charleston, South Carolina, named Lionel Henry Kennedy sentenced Denmark Vesey, a free man of African descent, to death. Vesey was found guilty of plotting what could have been the largest insurrection involving enslaved persons in United States history. Kennedy accused Vesey not only of treason against the state but of "attempting to pervert the sacred words of God into a sanction for crimes of the blackest hue." In his sentencing statement, Kennedy, after quoting several passages from the Bible that he believed obviously supported slavery, declared that "on such texts comment is unnecessary." Yet, after delving deeply into hundreds of pages of court records and related documents written in the aftermath of Vesey's trial, it seems to me that comment on these texts is indeed necessary.

As I studied these documents, I found that prominent pro-slavery colleagues of Kennedy at the time had indeed offered extensive commentary on biblical texts. Both Vesey's prosecutors and his allies appealed to the Bible to either decry or justify the insurrection plot. The appeals to the Bible on both sides of the debate spark the central questions of this book: In what ways was the Bible invoked to shape how Denmark Vesey's plot would be remembered? Would it be remembered as the fulfillment of divine law, an example of divine deliverance, or as a cautionary tale of the consequences of improper religious instruction?

Before beginning research for this book, I did not know much about the life and death of Denmark Vesey. I had seen his name listed alongside those of other leaders of revolts, such as Nat Turner. But I did not know much else about Vesey aside from his name. My ignorance about him would have endured were it not for two unrelated events in 2015. At the time, I was working with Nyasha Junior on a book titled *Black Samson: The Untold Story of an American Icon*. We wondered whether there were comparisons between Denmark Vesey and the biblical character Samson but found little evidence in the court documents and other primary sources from the 1820s that Vesey's contemporaries connected him to Samson. Yet, in the course of this research, I became intrigued by the many ways the Bible was used to both justify and condemn Vesey's plot. In the midst of this work, on June 17, 2015, a white supremacist gunman whose name I will not include in this book entered Emanuel African Methodist Episcopal (AME) Church in Charleston, sat through the Wednesday evening Bible study, and afterward murdered the Reverend Clementa C. Pinckney, along with eight other attendees: Cynthia Marie Graham Hurd, Susie Jackson, Ethel Lee Lance, DePayne Middleton-Doctor, Tywanza Sanders, Daniel L. Simmons, Sharonda Coleman-Singleton, and Myra Thompson. The church in which Denmark Vesey served as a leader and offered interpretations of the Bible was the forerunner of Emanuel AME. The gunman had selected this church for its symbolic importance. As I began to develop plans for a book on Denmark Vesey and the Bible, I became increasingly aware of how the events surrounding Vesey's life and death cast a shadow extending well into the early twenty-first century.

Over the past few decades, scholars have written several very informative books dealing with religion, the Bible, and slavery in the United States. Yet, helpful as these books may be, they tend to mention Vesey only briefly, if at all.[1] That said, this book is neither a biography of Denmark Vesey nor a historical reconstruction of the events related to Vesey's plot in Charleston in 1822.[2] Nor does this book try to determine *who* among those involved in the events surrounding Vesey's plot interpreted the Bible correctly or incorrectly. Rather, this book is about *how* various parties used the Bible to interpret the plot and define Vesey's legacy in the immediate aftermath of his trial and execution.

Admittedly, understanding how Vesey and his supporters used the Bible is difficult, because people who supported slavery produced all of the surviving primary source material from the immediate aftermath of Vesey's plot, his trial, and his execution. There is no extant written record about these events produced by Vesey or his supporters. Nor is there any direct evidence from the early 1820s in the archives about Vesey from people of African descent. At best, we have court testimony by witnesses of African descent recorded by slaveholders. Even if, for the sake of argument, we assume that the court magistrates recorded the witnesses' statements accurately, their testimony was in all likelihood coerced. Independent of the materials produced by white slaveholders, no written evidence exists from the 1820s for how people of African descent used the Bible to interpret Vesey's plot and define his legacy.

The slaveholders' extensive writings related to Vesey from the early 1820s provide much more documentation of their own use of the Bible to condemn his plot than of Vesey's use of it to support his plot. All we know of Vesey's biblical interpretations come in piecemeal fashion from the problematic court records, private letters, and newspaper articles written by slaveholders. No writings by Vesey survive, and no contemporary sermons

advocating for his cause remain. By contrast, the biblical interpretations of his slaveholding opponents survive in published
court records, pamphlets, sermons, and newspaper articles.
Given Vesey's involvement in the local church, I have no doubt
that his various uses of the Bible in support of his plot or sermons preached by other persons of African descent in the aftermath of his plot far exceed the few references that remain
today to how he interpreted the Bible. As I wrote this book, the
lopsided amount of surviving documentation frustrated me
greatly. When I began the research for this project, I did not
intend for the majority of the book to be about the hateful proslavery biblical interpretations of Vesey's opponents. I consider
it a shortcoming that its contents are as lopsided as the surviving documentary record. My hope is that as research related to
this subject matter develops and documentation for it improves,
future scholarship will be able to focus more directly on biblical
interpretations by Denmark Vesey himself as well as his contemporary supporters.

I have curtailed my references to secondary scholarship and
have focused instead on primary sources. The notes at the end
of the book will provide the interested reader with a representative sample of the contemporary scholarship that informs my
research. The notes could almost serve as a separate book in and
of themselves. In addition to scholarly references, the endnotes
contain a great deal of background information, detailed expla-
nations, and further source material that would break the flow
of the narrative if it appeared in the main body or as footnotes.
I would nonetheless strongly encourage readers to consult the
endnotes as they read the main body of the book for a more
nuanced appreciation of Denmark Vesey and his controversial
legacy. All biblical quotations in this book come from the King

James Version, as this was the translation used in all of the primary source material.

The introduction provides a basic overview of what we know about Vesey's life and the events surrounding his alleged plot, the trials of the accused, and their executions. Unavoidably, there will be references to many obscure events, names, and dates throughout this book. This can get a bit dense at points. To make it easier for readers to keep track of the major events, names, and dates that I reference, I have provided a list of major figures and a timeline of the major events discussed. Readers will also find in the back of this book an appendix containing a brief biographical sketch of Vesey's life, which appeared in the first published collection of court documents in August 1822. The appendix also includes transcripts of three death sentences handed down by the court against Denmark Vesey and others accused of conspiring with him.

ACKNOWLEDGMENTS

Several colleagues supported this project in various ways, including Blake Couey, Curtis Evans, Jeremy Hutton, Tod Linafelt, Seth Perry, Jeffrey Stackert, and Steven Weitzman. Fred Rowland, librarian at Temple University; Autumn Bennett, archives librarian at the College of Charleston; and Mary Jo Fairchild, manager of research services at the College of Charleston, helped me track down important documents during my research. Douglas R. Egerton not only provided invaluable feedback on this project, but also access to unpublished documents related to Vesey as well as Doug's own scholarship prior to its publication. As the COVID-19 pandemic restricted travel, I do not know if I could have written this book were it not for his generosity. My debt to Doug is apparent from the many references to his research throughout the book. I have met with Stephen C. Russell almost weekly to write together for several years. He has been part of the project since its inception. He was always willing to let me talk through ideas for this book with him as we wrote and studied in various coffee shops.

This book was funded in part by a John Simon Guggenheim Fellowship and the Presidential Humanities and Arts Research Program at Temple University, where I taught for 15 years. Slightly different versions of parts of this book appeared in my articles "'Misconstruction of the Sacred Page': On Denmark Vesey's Biblical Interpretations," *Journal of Biblical Literature* 138 (2019):

23–38; and "'On Such Texts Comment Is Unnecessary': Biblical Interpretation in the Trial of Denmark Vesey," *Journal of the American Academy of Religion* 85 (2017): 1032–49. I also presented a portion of this book as a talk titled "'Crimes of the Blackest Hue': Biblical Exegesis in the Trial of Denmark Vesey" at the University of Chicago Divinity School in May 2017.

Nyasha Junior is on my side. Whenever I lost confidence and became a hostile reader of my own writing, she would not abide such lazy thoughts or self-absorbed feelings. Instead, she would simply tell me to go back and write a better book. If this book has improved since its early drafts, it is because I revised it with the unshakable assurance that, without fanfare or hyperbole, Nyasha is in my corner. Every day.

I dedicate this book to my brothers, Tim and James Schipper, for the many unstated but enduring reasons that still make us a family during all the changes in our homes that we have celebrated and have mourned as we navigate our midlife years.

Introduction

CRIMES OF THE BLACKEST HUE

I am black, but comely.

—SONG OF SOLOMON 1:5

Moments before his execution on July 26, 1822, Jack Purcell exclaimed, "If it had not been for the cunning of that old villain Vesey, I should not now be in my present situation."[1] Purchased and enslaved by Ann Smith Bonsell Purcell of Charleston, South Carolina, Jack was one of the twenty-two men hanged that day for participating in a massive plot to liberate enslaved persons. Allegedly, the conspirators had planned to seize a cache of weapons from the local armory, set fires around Charleston, slaughter the city's white population, and escape to Haiti.[2] But the plot was uncovered and suppressed before it could get started. On July 2, three weeks before the mass executions, Denmark Vesey, the alleged leader of the plot, was hanged along with five enslaved men accused of being his fellow ringleaders. Still others were hanged on July 12, July 30, and August 9. In total, 131 people of African descent were arrested, 37 were banished, and 35 were executed.[3]

Vesey's plot could have led to the largest insurrection against slaveholders in the history of the United States. According to court records, the organizers anticipated that an army of thousands would join them. On July 25, 1822, one day before Jack Purcell's execution, Mary Lamboll Beach, a local slaveholding widow, wrote to her sister Elizabeth L. Gilchrist. In the letter, she explains how Jack came to join Vesey's conspiracy. According to Beach, he resisted Vesey's recruitment efforts at first, but then, "Vesey again came to him & with the Bible to quote different passages to prove the lawfulness of it."[4] Beach wrote several letters to her sister that summer. In a letter dated July 5, 1822, three days after Vesey was hanged, she described the contents of confiscated documents related to the plot, particularly those alluding to the biblical stories of the Israelites' exodus from Egypt and Samson's struggles against the Philistines. In these documents, she explained, the alleged conspirators "speak of their cause as one they expect the Lord will assist them in as he did the Israelites from their Master's & speak of their deliverance from the hand of the Philistines."[5] In the same letter, Beach claimed that after Vesey's arrest she was told that "the Negroes were under the impression that Denmark Vesey the free black *would* be delivered & if in *no* other way the Jail doors opened by a Supernatural Power."[6] This statement alludes to the New Testament story of Paul and Silas's miraculous deliverance from prison: "And at midnight Paul and Silas prayed, and sang praises unto God: and the prisoners heard them. And suddenly there was a great earthquake, so that the foundations of the prison were shaken: and immediately all the doors were opened, and every one's bands were loosed" (Acts 16:26). Beach goes on to describe how Vesey spent his final hours immersed in the psalms, singing like his imprisoned biblical counterparts Paul and Silas. "I heard that Vesey said in the Jail that it was a Glorious cause he was to die in & the singing of the Psalms &cc in there the night before was carried on to a *great* extent."[7] Within days of Vesey's death, Beach used biblical texts as a prism through which she interpreted the aspirations of the leader of the suppressed plot.

One of the more effective ways that Vesey was able to recruit people like Jack Purcell to his cause was through his impassioned appeals to the Bible. At the trials of those accused of involvement in Vesey's plot, several witnesses testified that he read from the Bible at planning meetings held at his house. Rolla Bennett, who was enslaved by South Carolina Governor Thomas Bennett Jr., was one of the five alleged ringleaders executed alongside Vesey on the fateful day of July 2. According to court documents, he confessed during his own trial that Vesey *"read to us from the Bible, how the Children of Israel were delivered out of Egypt from bondage."*[8] As I discuss in chapter 1, Rolla's allusion to a biblical text does not identify it by chapter or verse but uses language that appears in several biblical texts related to the story of Israelites' deliverance from slavery in Egypt. Even if Rolla could not identify the exact biblical text that Vesey read, references to this story occur frequently in early African American literature.[9] Jesse Blackwood was another of the five ringleaders who died alongside Vesey. Jesse, who was enslaved by a local bank president named Thomas Blackwood, allegedly confessed after he was sentenced to death. He claimed that during a planning meeting at Vesey's house, Vesey instructed those present to kill the white men, women, and children of Charleston "for he said, God had so commanded it in the scriptures."[10] The first witness in Vesey's trial was a man named William Paul, who was enslaved by a local grocer named John Paul. On June 19, William testified that Vesey "studies all he can to put it into the heads of the blacks to have a rising against the whites."[11] William elaborated, "he studies the Bible a great deal and tries to prove from it that slavery and bondage is against the Bible."[12]

Vesey was not alone in appealing to the Bible at these meetings. Jacob Glen, also known as Jack, was enslaved by a planter named John S. Glen and was one of the twenty-two enslaved men executed on July 26. Charleston's mayor, James Hamilton Jr., identified Jacob as "a Preacher."[13] At Jacob's trial, Charles Drayton, a cook who was enslaved by former South Carolina governor, John Drayton, testified that during a meeting at Vesey's house Jacob "quoted Scripture to prove he would not be condemned for raising against the Whites."[14] Similarly, Bacchus Hammet, who was enslaved by a merchant named Benjamin Hammet, testified, "I saw Jack [Jacob] at Vesey's the first time I met there—he was the man who read the Bible—he passed the hat round that night for the contribution."[15] Bacchus's testimony did not save his life. He was hanged on the same day as Jack Purcell, Jacob Glen, and many others.

William Paul also read from the Bible during planning meetings. During the trial of Mingo Harth, who was enslaved by a lumber merchant named William Harth, William Paul testified, "At Mingo's house I took up the Bible and read two chapters from the prophet Tobit."[16] Others alluded to well-known biblical passages even if they did not read from them directly. Joe La Roche, who was enslaved by a local widow named Mary La Roche, described how he cited one of the Ten Commandments when resisting Rolla's repeated efforts to recruit him. La Roche explained, "About three months ago he asked me to join with him in slaying the whites, I asked him to give me time to consider of it." He continued, "he again came to me on the same subject. I told him 'take care, God says we must not kill.'" Whether he knew the exact origins of this divine command, La Roche alludes to Exodus 20:13 and Deuteronomy 5:17, which the King James Version renders as "Thou shalt not kill." Several decades later, Archibald Henry Grimké wrote a twenty-four-page history of Vesey's plot titled *Right on the Scaffold: or, The Martyrs of 1822.*[17] Grimké was a Harvard-educated lawyer and vice president of the National Association for the Advancement of Colored People (NAACP) who was born into slavery in Charleston. "He [Vesey] ransacked the Bible for apposite and terrible texts," Grimké vividly declared, "whose commands in the olden times, to the olden people, were no less imperative upon the new times and the new people [i.e., people of African descent in Charleston]."[18]

Vesey's extensive engagement with the Bible did not go unnoticed by those presiding at his trial. Lionel Henry Kennedy, a Yale-educated lawyer and representative in the South Carolina legislature who, at the time of his death, held twenty-two persons in slavery, was a presiding magistrate of the first court organized for the trials of those allegedly involved in the plot.[19] When sentencing Vesey to death, Kennedy went beyond the formal charge of "attempting to raise an Insurrection amongst the Blacks against the Whites."[20] To Vesey, he sternly remarked, "In addition to treason, you have committed the grossest impiety, in attempting to pervert the sacred words of God into a sanction for crimes of the blackest hue."[21] Kennedy and presumably the other members of the court were shocked and appalled by how Vesey had found support for his plot in the pages of the Bible. Over the next several months, the slaveholding elites in Charleston would write letters, print newspaper editorials and pamphlets, preach sermons, and publish trial transcripts that included biblical defenses of slavery. The legitimacy of Vesey's plot quickly became a matter of serious and detailed biblical interpretation.

Denmark Vesey's Bible survives as an idea but not as a document. Official court records report, "Vesey had a variety of papers and books relating to this transaction [the plot], *which he burnt when the discovery of the intended attempt was made.*"[22] Witnesses at the trials claimed that the alleged ringleaders kept lists of the names of those committed to the insurrection. In a confession dated July 12, Bacchus Hammet allegedly stated that at one meeting "a large Book like a Bible was open before them at Denmarks house" but that he did "not know whether it was to sign names in or what purpose."[23] If Vesey kept a list of his co-conspirators in his Bible, it is possible his Bible was among the many books and papers that Vesey destroyed once the plot was uncovered. Alternatively, he could have hidden his Bible, buried it, or given it to someone else for safekeeping, because some of the alleged conspirators buried supplies, including arms and powder. Bacchus Hammet also stated that he was told, "Gullah Jack had buried the powder, and I think Perault knows where it is."[24] In a letter from Lydia Maria Child, a prominent white abolitionist, to Thomas Wentworth Higginson, a Unitarian minister and abolitionist, dated March 17, 1860, decades after Vesey's death, Child recalled rumors that she "heard, at the time, of arms being buried in coffins."[25] The 1856 novel *Dred: A Tale of the Great Dismal Swamp* by the celebrated antislavery author Harriet Beecher Stowe, best known for her classic *Uncle Tom's Cabin*, features a fictional son of Vesey named Dred, whom Stowe imagines as inheriting and studying his father's Bible after his father's death.[26] Ultimately, we may never know what actually happened to Vesey's Bible. Since no writings from Vesey's own hand survive, we do not possess his own, firsthand interpretations of the Bible. All we have are biblical interpretations attributed to him at the trials in the summer of 1822— from the trial transcripts prepared by James Hamilton Jr.,

Charleston's intendant (or mayor), and by Lionel Henry Kennedy and Thomas Parker, the magistrates at Vesey's trial.

In mid-August 1822, Hamilton published some of the court documents as a forty-six-page pamphlet titled *An Account of the Late Intended Insurrection among a Portion of the Blacks of the City* (hereafter *Account*).[27] In October 1822, Kennedy and Parker published a more extensive version as the 202-page *An Official Report of the Trials of Sundry Negroes, Charged with an Attempt to Raise an Insurrection in the State of South-Carolina* (hereafter *Official Report*).[28] At the request of South Carolina Governor Thomas Bennett Jr., Kennedy and Parker also prepared trial transcripts for the South Carolina House of Representatives, docketed as "Document B House of Representatives" and a longer version for the South Carolina Senate, docketed as "Evidence Document B."[29] The transcription of these documents was not completed until November 1822.[30] All four versions of the court documents suggest that Vesey appealed to certain biblical texts to promote and justify his plot without, however, recording direct testimony from Vesey himself.

We know very little about the man behind the insurrection plot that rocked Charleston in the summer of 1822. Most of our information about Denmark Vesey's life comes from a 524-word footnote buried deep within Hamilton's *Account*. The footnote served as a primary source for early biographical sketches of Vesey. In 1849, Henry Bibb, a prominent abolitionist who escaped slavery in Kentucky, published *Slave Insurrection in 1831, in Southampton County, VA., Headed by Nat Turner, also a Conspiracy of Slaves, in Charleston, South Carolina, in 1822*, which relies heavily on Hamilton's footnote for its overview of Vesey's life.[31] The same is true for the biographical material in Grimké's *Right on the Scaffold* in 1901.[32] Grimké's account, in turn, served as the main source for other biographical sketches of Vesey by African American intellectuals in the early twentieth century, such as Benjamin Griffith Brawley, a Harvard-educated writer and the first dean of Morehouse College, or the famed sociologist W.E.B. DuBois.[33]

In all likelihood, Joseph Vesey, Denmark's former slaveholder, was Hamilton's source of information for Hamilton's biographical footnote, since he was still living in Charleston in the summer of 1822. A native of Bermuda, Joseph Vesey commanded a ship that sailed between St. Thomas and Saint-Domingue before he settled in Charleston. During one of his voyages in 1781, he transported 390 enslaved persons to Saint-Domingue. Among them was a young man thought to be about fourteen years old. According to Hamilton, he had a "beauty, alertness and intelligence" that caught the attention of Captain Vesey and his officers. Once aboard, they took him to the ship's cabin, changed his clothes, and renamed him Telemaque (there is no record of his earlier name). But when the ship reached Saint-Domingue, Telemaque was sold along with the other enslaved men, women, and children.

That would have been the end of his story if Telemaque had not been returned to Joseph Vesey upon his next trip to Saint-Domingue in the spring of 1782. According to Hamilton's account, the planter who had purchased Telemaque said that he was "unsound, and subject to epileptic fits." Some have speculated that Telemaque feigned these seizures to avoid a lifetime of forced labor on a planation because, by local law, enslaved persons who were imported had to be disease-free. Otherwise, the purchasers could return them to the seller. We may never know whether the young man feigned his illness, but there is

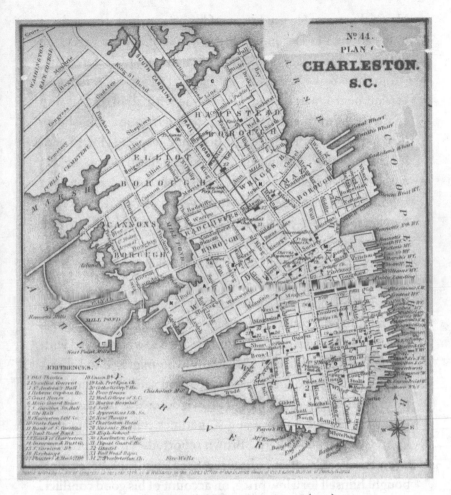

FIGURE 1. Map titled "Plan of Charleston" (1849).

no evidence that Telemaque had epilepsy or any other severe health conditions before or after those few months in Saint-Domingue.[34] Telemaque remained enslaved by Joseph Vesey when the ship captain settled in Charleston.

Telemaque's life changed dramatically in Charleston when he "drew a prize of $1500 in the East-Bay-Street Lottery" in

November 1799. He used $600 of his prize money to purchase his freedom. On December 31, 1799, Mary Clodner Vesey, the wife of Joseph Vesey, had papers drawn up which stated that "from the yoke of Servitude" she had "set free and discharged a certain negro man named Telemaque with all his goods and chattel."[35] With the remaining $900, Telemaque established a thriving carpentry business and became a respected member of his community.[36] "Among his colour," Hamilton wrote, "he was always looked up to with awe and respect." As a free man, he retained the surname Vesey but eventually abandoned the name given to him on the slave ship in favor of a variation used by those of African descent in Charleston. As Hamilton explained, "among the negroes," the name Telemaque was eventually "changed to Denmark, or sometimes Telmak."

Court documents identify Vesey as "a free black man" but do not mention his country of origin.[37] Thomas Cilavan Brown, a free man of African descent, was a carpenter who worked with Vesey. He was a native of Charleston who migrated to Liberia before returning to the United States and settling in Philadelphia. Years after Vesey's death, Brown described him to Lydia Maria Child. "Denmark Vesey, sometimes called Telemachus, was a Corromantee negro," Brown reported. "He was brought from the [gold] coast [of west Africa] by Capt Vesey, and bought himself for a low price, on account of his good conduct. He was a large, stout man."[38] As historians Douglas R. Egerton and Robert L. Paquette explain, "Enslaved Africans from the Gold Coast were often called, with variant spellings, Coromantee, after an English trading post created there in the seventeenth century."[39] Because Joseph Vesey imported enslaved persons from west Africa and St. Thomas, Denmark Vesey could have been born in Africa rather than the Caribbean. Unfortunately, no record of his birthplace survives. Later sources refer to Vesey as "a mulatto from Saint Domingo," but this claim conflicts with our earliest evidence.[40]

——————

When sentencing Vesey to death, Kennedy was dumbstruck that Vesey would have even attempted to organize an insurrection. Somewhat stupefied, he exclaimed, "It is difficult to imagine what *infatuation* could have prompted you to attempt an enterprize so wild and visionary. You were a free man; were comparatively wealthy; and enjoyed every comfort, compatible with your situation. You had, therefore, much to risk, and little to gain. From your age and experience, you *ought* to have known, that success was impracticable."[41] Yet, his family situation as well as certain political and religious developments over the previous several years, may have also convinced Vesey that the insurrection's time had come.

Vesey had married three times (to Beck, Dolly, and then Susan) and had fathered multiple children. Despite the income from his lottery winnings and his carpentry business, he did not have enough money to purchase freedom for his enslaved family members. According to a confession by Monday Gell, an enslaved harness-maker who provided the court with the names of forty-two alleged conspirators several days after Vesey and the five other accused ringleaders were executed, Vesey's desire for insurrection was driven by a concern for his family. Sometime in mid-July, Monday informed the court: "Vesey said he was satisfied with his own condition, being free, but as all his children were slaves, he wished to see what could be done for them."[42]

In 1820, the United States Congress reached what became known as the Missouri Compromise. Missouri's request for admission to the Union as a slaveholding state was granted on the condition that Maine be granted admission as a state in which slavery was prohibited. At the time, Rufus King, an influential senator from New York, was among the fiercest opponents of slavery in Congress. His passionate speeches on the Senate floor were circulated throughout the United States. They made their way to Charleston and, eventually, into the hands of Denmark Vesey. In addition to the Bible, Vesey used these speeches to persuade others to join the conspiracy. For example, in the aforementioned confession that Jack Purcell gave shortly before his execution, he claimed that Vesey would read to him from various newspaper articles. "He one day brought me a speech which he told me had been delivered in Congress by a *Mr. King* on the subject of slavery; he told me this Mr. King was the black man's friend."[43] In their introductory narrative to the *Official Report*, Kennedy and Parker claim that by appealing to these speeches, Vesey "persuaded but too many that Congress had actually declared them free, and that they were held in bondage contrary to the laws of the land."[44] According to Kennedy and Parker, Vesey used biblical texts to convince Jack of the divine endorsement of the insurrection and Senator King's speeches to convince him of the unlawfulness of slavery.

The establishment of what became known as the African Church in Charleston a few years earlier also played an important role in the timing of Vesey's plot. In 1816, Morris Brown, a free mixed-race native of Charleston, and Henry Drayton, a formerly enslaved mixed-race man, traveled to Philadelphia to meet with Richard Allen, a founder and the first bishop of the African Methodist Episcopal Church.[45] Shortly after their return to Charleston, two independent African Methodist churches were built in the city. These churches, commonly referred to as the African Church at the time, would become the forerunner of the historic Emanuel African Methodist Episco-

FIGURE 2. Emanuel African Methodist Episcopal Church (present day).

pal Church. In 1817, over four thousand congregants of African descent left the Methodist church led by white clergy in Charleston. In 1830, James Osgood Andrew, a local slaveholding clergyman at the Trinity Methodist Church, wrote a brief history of Methodism in Charleston in which he provided a vivid description of services in the aftermath of this mass departure. "In the galleries, once crowded with attentive and prayerful hearers, now only a few faces were seen; and instead of the full chorus of happy voices, which used to hymn the praises of God, the preacher was called to witness a silent and mournful solitude."[46]

But soon after the African Church opened its doors, Charleston's white slaveholding elites viewed it as fostering antislavery sentiments among those of African descent. On Sunday, June 7, 1818, the City Guard disrupted services and arrested 143 free and enslaved persons of African descent. Two years later, over one hundred white citizens signed a petition to the South Carolina legislature, dated October 16, 1820, which called for further restrictions on people of African descent. Among other stated concerns, the petition warned that the African Church in Charleston was supported by "Abolition Societies in the Eastern and Northern States."

Your petitioners beg leave to invite the attention of the Legislature to other existing evils, in communicating which they have first to state, that a spacious Building has lately been erected in the immediate neighbourhood of Charleston for the *exclusive* worship of Negroes and coloured people, from means supplied them by Abolition Societies in the Eastern and Northern States, as your petitioners are credibly informed, this Establishment is no less impolitick than unnecessary in as much as ample accommodation is, and has always been provided and afforded the Negroes and coloured people in the numerous Churches and places of Publick worship in the City of Charleston and its neighbourhood.[47]

Although this petition does not provide specifics about the religious practices or instruction in the African Church, it shows concerns over worship unsupervised by white people. The suspicion that the African Methodist Episcopal Church and antislavery missionaries in Philadelphia unduly influenced the African Church grew among Charleston's white elites once Vesey's plot was discovered. On June 29, 1822, the day after Denmark Vesey's conviction, a local merchant and banker named John Porter wrote to Langdon Cleves, a former South Carolina congressman who was serving as the president of the Second Bank of the United States in Philadelphia at the time. "Their meetings Commenced, and were held under the perfidious Cover of Religion—and I cannot doubt," Porter declared, "they were aided by the black missionaries from *Your City!*"[48] A few months later, on September 23, the board of the Charleston Bible Society drafted a letter (which I discuss further in chapter 5) to Governor Thomas Bennett Jr., echoing Porter's claim: "the most leading Characters among [those involved in Vesey's plot], & the chief of the rest, were members of an irregular Association, which called itself the African Church, & was intimately connected with a similar Body in Philadelphia, from which their sentiments & directions in Matters of Religion were chiefly derived."[49]

According to the records of Charleston's Second Presbyterian Church, Vesey was one of "three people of Colour" admitted to the congregation's communion on April 12, 1817. At the time, this was not unusual, considering that a report of the board of managers of the local Bible Society of Charleston estimated that by 1819 "one-fourth of the communicants of the Presbyterian churches of Charleston were colored."[50] Unlike the other two new congregants of color, however, Vesey was not baptized on that day, and there is no further record of his involvement with the Second Presbyterian Church. Sometime within the next few years, Vesey became actively involved in the African Church, which Hamilton referred to as "a hot-bed, in which the germ [of Vesey's plot] might well be expected to spring into life and vigour." Hamilton further noted, "Among the conspirators a majority of them belonged to the *African Church* and among those executed were several who had been Class Leaders."[51]

A system of "class leaders" in local Methodist churches facilitated gatherings of free or enslaved people of African descent. In addition to Sunday services, classes were held on weekday evenings, led by a lay "coloured preacher or leader," as explained in the introductory narrative in the *Official Report*. Kennedy and Parker crafted their description to suggest that these meetings were dangerously radical events held under the guise of religious instruction. The class meetings were "held usually at night in some retired building, avowedly for religious instruction and worship." As "no white person attended," Kennedy and Parker surmised, "they were to be used as places of rendezvous and rallying points, for communicating to all, the exact night and hour, on which the first blow was to be struck."[52] Martha Proctor Richardson, a white widow living in Savannah, Georgia, wrote a letter, dated Saturday, July 6, 1822, to James Screven, her nephew and future plantation owner in Charleston.[53] Referring to Vesey and those who died with him, she informed Screven, "Six were condemned and executed on 2d July—it is said that the leaders in this conspiracy were class leaders of religious societies." A few lines later she reiterated, "The Ring

Leaders of the conspiracy were all of them Class Leaders or Deacons."[54] This assertion is corroborated in part by testimony during the trial of Mingo Harth, when William Paul claimed, "Peter, Ned and Charles I know to be class leaders in the African Church."[55] As observed earlier, several witnesses testified about class meetings held in Vesey's home.

By mid-August 1822, the African Church in Charleston was razed and sold off for lumber, or, in the words of Hamilton, "voluntarily dissolved."[56] Morris Brown and Henry Drayton were forced into exile. On August 6, 1822, Judge John B. White ruled that Brown and Drayton had violated an 1821 South Carolina law prohibiting free persons of African descent from leaving and then returning to the state. Judge White declared, "I do hereby order the said Morris Brown and Henry Drayton, to leave this State within fifteen days from this date, under the pains and penalties which await them in case of their disobedience."[57] Brown fled to Philadelphia, where he would eventually become the second bishop of the African Methodist Episcopal Church, succeeding Richard Allen.

———

It was the afternoon of May 22, 1822. Peter Prioleau, a mixed-race cook who was enslaved by Colonel John Cordes Prioleau, was returning from the market when he was approached by William Paul. After some initial small talk, William cut to the chase. "Do you know that something serious is about to take place?" he asked, "many of us are determined to right ourselves!"[58] When Peter pressed him for details, William replied, "if you will go with me, I will show you the man, who has the list of names who will take yours down."[59] But Peter resisted. Later, he testified, "I would have nothing to do with this business, that

I was satisfied with my condition, that I was grateful to my master for his kindness and wished no change."[60] After consulting with William Penceel, a free man who belonged to the Brown Society Fellowship, a mutual aid organization whose members identified as "mulatto," Peter decided to inform his slaveholder. When Colonel Prioleau returned from out-of-town business a few days later, Peter told him about the plot. The information was passed along to James Hamilton, who ordered the arrest of William Paul. When interrogated, William implicated Mingo Harth and Paul Poyas. On May 31, Mingo and Paul were questioned but released.

Just over a week later, on June 9, Joe La Roche and Ned Bennett attempted unsuccessfully to recruit George Wilson, a class leader in the African Church who was enslaved by Major John Wilson. Five days later, George told his slaveholder of the plot. Major Wilson informed Hamilton, who then informed Governor Bennett. The next day, Governor Bennett ordered the arrests of Mingo Harth, Paul Poyas, and Rolla Bennett. Initially, the governor was skeptical about the allegations, but after Rolla confessed, the militia was deployed.

Out of all the witnesses at the trials, Monday Gell stood out. In his *Account*, Hamilton declared, "It would be difficult to name any individual more actively engaged in the plot than [Monday], or more able to aid Denmark Vesey, from his uncommon sagacity and knowledge."[61] After his conviction, Monday was offered a reduced sentence of banishment rather than death in exchange for his confessions. According to Monday, Vesey had originally intended the insurrection to take place on July 14. Vesey, who spoke French, probably selected this date because it was Bastille Day, the celebration of the storming of the Bastille during the French Revolution. Monday told the court, "*Vesey originally proposed the second Sunday, or the 14th of*

July, as the day for rising, but afterwards changed it to the 16th of June."[62] Yet, when the new date arrived, an alleged ringleader named Jack Pritchard informed others that the timetable was to be delayed. Jack, who was enslaved by Paul Pritchard, was one of Vesey's close associates. He was also known as Gullah Jack or sometimes Couter Jack. As Yorrick Cross, who was enslaved by Vesey's attorney George W. Cross, testified at Jack's trial, "On that day he [Jack] came to me and said they would not break out that night as the patrol was too strong."[63] Jack was hanged on July 12.

After Peter Prioleau and George Wilson betrayed those involved in Vesey's plot, a series of arrests followed quickly. On June 19, Hamilton organized a Court of Magistrates and Free-holders with Lionel Henry Kennedy and Thomas Parker serving as magistrates. On June 22, William Dove, the captain of the City Guard, arrested Vesey. On June 27, the court tried Vesey. On June 28, Kennedy sentenced Vesey to death. On July 2, 1822, Denmark Vesey was hanged.

Since the mid-nineteenth century, interpreters of Vesey's plot have focused on Kennedy and Parker's *Official Report* as a primary source from which to reconstruct Vesey's use of biblical texts. In her novel *Dred: A Tale of the Great Dismal Swamp*, Stowe quotes from the *Official Report* directly to support her claim that Vesey's "great instrument of influence was a book that has always been prolific in insurrectionary movements, under all systems of despotism."[64] In 1861, Thomas Wentworth Higginson wrote an influential article in the *Atlantic Monthly* that also quoted from Kennedy and Parker when discussing Vesey's biblical interpretation.[65]

Even Grimké's *Right on the Scaffold* relied on Kennedy and Parker's summary of Vesey's favorite biblical texts. Grimké explained that Vesey interpreted a verse from the book of Joshua as applicable to those of African descent in Charleston. Like their ancient Israelite counterparts, they were "also commanded to arise and destroy their enemies and the city in which they dwelt 'both man and woman, young and old, . . . with the edge of the sword' [Joshua 6:21]."[66] Grimké continues, "He looked confidently for a day of vengeance and retribution for the blacks. He felt . . . in the stern and exultant prophecy of Zachariah, fierce and sanguinary words, which were constantly in his mouth 'Then shall the Lord go forth, and fight against those nations, as when he fought in the day of battle' [Zechariah 14:3]. According to Vesey's lurid exegesis 'those nations' meant, beyond a peradventure, the cruel masters."[67] Grimké's comments and biblical quotations are consistent with what Kennedy and Parker write in the *Official Report*, as is discussed in the next chapter.

All of the trial transcripts that Kennedy and Parker prepared for publication use the King James Version of the Bible, even when recording the testimony or statements made by witnesses at the trials. For example, according to their transcription of a confession, John Enslow, who was enslaved by a cooper named Joseph Enslow, quoted from the King James Version by chapter and verse. He stated, "Denmark had several Meetings at different times, he generally opened them by reading the 21st Chapter of *Exodus* and exhorting them from the 16th verse; he that Stealeth a man and Selleth, or if he be found in his hands shall surely be put to death."[68] Nevertheless, the biblical translations used by Vesey and his associates were not necessarily limited to the King James Version. As mentioned earlier, William Paul testified that he read from the book of Tobit during a meeting at Mingo Harth's home. Tobit is found among the fourteen Apocryphal or Deuterocanonical books, which are not included in most Protestant editions of the King James Version. William did not indicate whether the Bible from which he read belonged to Mingo, Vesey, or someone else. Moreover, local newspapers advertised the availability of Bibles with the Apocrypha.[69] So it is entirely possible that whoever owned that particular Bible, regardless of her or his particular church affiliation, just happened to acquire one with the Apocrypha, since they were readily available in Charleston at the time.

Vesey and his associates may have read from the Apocrypha, but the biblical texts that they cited to support the insurrection came largely from the Old Testament.[70] Yet, although many of the biblical texts that Charleston's white elites used to defend slavery came from the New Testament Epistles, Vesey and his associates also utilized a few texts from the New Testament. According to the testimony of Monday Gell, a meeting was held at the home of a man identified only as Philip. Philip was a preacher who would quote from John 14:27 ("Let not your heart be troubled, neither let it be afraid") to encourage recruits whose resolve was wavering. "It is probable that the timid and the wavering were brought [presumably by Vesey or one of his associates] to this High Priest of sedition, to be confirmed in good resolutions," Kennedy and Parker speculated, "and would then shew how applicable the text was 'let not thy heart be troubled, neither be afraid.'"[71] An 1823 proslavery pamphlet by Frederick Dalcho, discussed in detail in chapter 6, alleges that one of men executed for his participation in the plot used John 14 as a source of comfort. Dalcho exclaims, "one of the convicts, the day before his execution, was overheard expounding to his wife, the beginning of the 14th chapter of St. John, and applying it to himself. It was necessary, he said, that he should go to prepare a place in heaven for his wife!"[72] In the introductory narrative to the *Official Report*, Kennedy and Parker claim that Vesey and his colleagues used a verse from the Gospel of Luke as their creed, although none of the witnesses in the trials mentions this text. Kennedy and Parker write, "the City was to have been fired, and an indiscriminate slaughter of the whites to commence, and also of those of their own colour who had not joined them, or did not immediately do so. It was determined that no one should be neuter; 'he that is not with me is against me' [Luke 11:23] was their creed."[73]

As I discuss throughout this book, whereas Charleston's white elites often drew clear distinctions between Old and New Testament texts in their proslavery arguments, for whatever reasons, Vesey and his associates did not make these distinctions as precisely, if at all. This may be because many of Vesey's associates, with varying degrees of literacy, may have had recent or limited exposure to the various Christian orderings of biblical material. Most likely, however, it simply did not matter to Vesey and his associates where in the Bible a text was located if the text proved useful for their cause. In addition to the Bible, Vesey and his associates made use of other texts or religious practices that could convince recruits to join them or strengthen the resolve of those already committed to their cause.[74] When necessary, Vesey resorted to classic Greek mythology to persuade others to join his plot. At Vesey's trial, Joe La Roche testified that they met each other on the road one day and Vesey asked him if he was satisfied with his present situation. Vesey then asked if he "remembered the fable of Hercules and the Waggoner whose waggon was stalled, and he began to pray, and Hercules said, you fool put your shoulders to the wheel, whip up the horses and your waggon will be pulled out." The moral of the story, Vesey concluded, was "that if we did not put our hand to the work and deliver ourselves, we should never come out of slavery."[75]

Jack Pritchard, also known as Gullah Jack, helped to recruit others to Vesey's cause. As discussed in chapter 3, Jack allegedly used traditional African religious and medical practices to encourage his recruits instead of appeals to biblical texts. At the same time, Kennedy and Parker list Jack among the members of the African Church in their introductory narrative to the *Official Report* when they note, "Vesey had been a member, and of which his principal associates, Gullah Jack, Monday, Ned and Peter, were also members."[76] This suggests that Vesey and his associates did not base their religious appeals strictly on the Bible and Christianity. Rather, as historian Margaret Washington has argued, Gullah religious practices were "integrating the old ways [traditional African religious practices] into Christianity."[77] There is no evidence that Vesey and his associates only recruited among Christians or that they drew a strict division between traditional African religious and medical practices and Christianity. Instead, as historian Eugene Genovese has observed, Vesey was "formulating a flexible religious appeal" based on "both African and classical Christian ideas and appeals." Genovese continues, "Denmark Vesey most creatively captured the complex tradition of the people he sought to lead."[78] Nevertheless, Charleston's white legal and religious authorities often depicted this complex tradition as either naïve, unchristian superstition or as a malevolent misinterpretation of Christian scripture. For example, Kennedy and Parker refer to Philip, the preacher mentioned earlier who quoted John 14:27, as the "High Priest of sedition," presumably because Philip also seemed to have utilized traditional African religious practices.[79]

———

Biographers often remember Vesey through the prism of biblical language—a language Vesey himself invoked and that has been used repeatedly to describe him and his mission. Written nearly eighty years after Vesey's death, Grimké's 1901 biography opens with a reference to a line from Song of Solomon 1:5: "He was black but comely."[80] Grimké's citation of this biblical verse does more than simply provide a racial identification for Vesey, since Grimké refers to Vesey as "black" without a reference to the Bible throughout his biography.[81] This opening imbues with biblical significance Hamilton's earlier claim that, as a young man, Vesey had "beauty, alertness and intelligence." It also connects Vesey with a tradition, well established by the end of the nineteenth century, of using Song of Solomon 1:5 to celebrate the lives and accomplishments of people of African descent.[82] A full century later, in what is to date the definitive scholarly biography of Denmark Vesey, Egerton does something similar. The title of this biography, *He Shall Go Out Free*, comes from Exodus 21:2 ("If thou buy an Hebrew servant, six years he shall serve: and in the seventh he shall go out free for nothing").[83] Several of the Egerton's chapter titles also come from the Bible: chapter 2, "Stranger in a Strange Land" (Exodus 2:22); chapter 5, "Building the House of the Lord" (1 Kings 9:1); chapter 6, "Exodus"; chapter 7, "Lamentations"; and chapter 8, "Judges." The Bible, in other words, served not only as a tool used by Vesey and his white supremacist adversaries to justify or condemn the insurrection plot in the 1820s. It provides the language through which, to this day, we continue to interpret the life and actions of the controversial and mysterious man at the center of the conspiracy.

CHAPTER ONE

He Shall Surely Be Put to Death

> He that stealeth a man, and selleth him, or if he be found in his
> hand, he shall surely be put to death.
>
> —EXODUS 21:16

Just two years before Denmark Vesey was admitted to Charleston's Second Presbyterian Church's communion in the spring of 1817, a debate over slavery had rocked the Presbyterian Church at the national level. In 1815, George Bourne, an English-born clergyman living in Virginia, was expelled from the ministry by his local presbytery. The expulsion was triggered by a public stance taken by Bourne earlier that year at the denomination's General Assembly meeting in Philadelphia. At the meeting, Bourne called attention to a statement buried deep within the Westminster Larger Catechism of 1647, a foundational document for the denomination. In response to question 142, the Catechism states, "The sins forbidden in the eighth commandment ["Thou shalt not steal"]," include "theft, robbery, man-stealing, and receiving anything that is stolen." Since the catechism considers "man-stealing" a violation of the eighth commandment, Bourne reasoned, Presbyterians should not condone slavery. Bourne's argument did not win the Assembly over, and when he returned home to Virginia, he was defrocked.

But Bourne was not deterred. The following year he published a fulsome condemnation of slavery titled *The Book and Slavery Irreconcilable*.[1] This landmark book wove together a wide array of biblical texts and commentaries by earlier theological authorities to show that slavery is a sin. For example, Bourne invoked John Wesley, the famed theologian and founder of Methodism. In the 1750s, decades before the Declaration of Independence, Wesley connected the transatlantic slave trade with biblical condemnations of "man-stealing." Bourne quoted Wesley's comments on 1 Timothy 1:10, which focused on the reference to "menstealers" in this verse.[2] "Man-stealers!" Wesley exclaimed, "The worst of all thieves; in comparison of whom, highway robbers and house-breakers are innocent! What then are traders in Negroes, and procurers of servants for America, and all who list soldiers by lies, tricks, or enticements?"[3] Bourne also cited Adam Clarke, an early Methodist theologian whose six-volume commentary on the Bible remained influential in Methodist circles well into the twentieth century. Bourne quotes Clarke's commentary on the severe penalty found in Exodus 21:16, which serves as this chapter's epigraph. "By this law" Clarke observes, "every man-stealer, and every receiver of the stolen person, should lose his life; no matter whether the latter stole the man himself, or gave money to a slave captain or negro-dealer to steal for him. All kidnapping and slave-dealing are prohibited, whether practiced by individuals or the state."[4]

———

Exodus 21:16 featured prominently in antislavery literature long before Bourne published *The Book and Slavery Irreconcilable*. A reference to this verse appears in the first publication of laws in colonial America. In 1641, Nathaniel Ward, an English Puritan minister who immigrated to Massachusetts, compiled the *Massachusetts Body of Liberties*. Although this document does not connect this passage to the practice of slavery explicitly, it cites the biblical text by chapter and verse, implying that it was authoritative in Massachusetts: "(Ex. 21. 16.) If any man stealeth a man or mankinde, he shall surely be put to death."[5]

On August 13, 1693, at a Quaker meeting in Philadelphia, George Keith implored his fellow Quakers to reject the practice of slavery. He argued that biblical law considers manstealing a far more serious offense than other types of stealing because it is punishable by death. He contrasted Exodus 21:16 with a law that appears several verses later. Exodus 21.1 (which is Exodus 21:37 in Hebrew) requires a person who steals and then kills an ox or a sheep to pay back the animal's owner with 5 oxen or 4 sheep, respectively. That stealing and even killing these animals is not punishable by death, Keith reasoned, shows that "perpetual Bondage and Slavery" is done "to the great scandal of the *Christian Profession*."[6] In 1700, Samuel Sewall connected Exodus 21:16 with the transatlantic slave trade directly. He wrote, "And seeing GOD hath said, *He that Stealeth a Man and Selleth him, or if he be found in his hand, he shall surely be put to Death*. Exod. 21.16. This Law being of Everlasting Equity, wherein Man Stealing is ranked amongst the most atrocious of Capital Crimes: What louder Cry can there be made of the Celebrated Warning."[7]

In 1782, the French-American author J. Hector St. John de Crèvecoeur published *Letters from an American Farmer*.[8] The book, structured as a series of twelve letters from a fictitious American farmer to an Englishman, enjoyed great popularity in Europe upon its publication.[9] Letter 9, titled "Description of Charles Town; Thoughts on Slavery; on Physical Evil; a Melancholy Scene," recounts the narrator's visit to Charleston. At the end of this letter, he describes in horrific detail how an enslaved man was left to die slowly in a cage for killing the overseer of the plantation on which he was forced to work. While *Letters from an American Farmer* was not initially as popular in America as in Europe, an excerpt of this story about the enslaved killer was reprinted five years later in the March 1787 issue of Philadelphia-based publication the *American Museum*.[10] The introduction to the excerpt begins by quoting Exodus 21:16, implying that the killing of the overseer was biblically justified.[11]

That same year (1787) in London, a formerly enslaved man named Ottobah Cugoano published a scathing critique of slavery titled *Thoughts and Sentiments on the Evil and Wicked Traffic of the Slavery and Commerce of the Human Species*. On the title page, Cugoano combined parts of Exodus 21:16 and Deuteronomy 24:7 to serve as the book's epigraph: "He that stealeth a man and selleth him, or maketh merchandize of him, or if he be found in his hand: then that thief shall die." In its entirety, Deuteronomy 24:7 reads, "If a man be found stealing any of his brethren of the children of Israel, and maketh merchandise of him, or selleth him; then that thief shall die; and thou shalt put evil away from among you." When combining this verse with Exodus 21:16, Cugoano does not include Deuteronomy's reference to "brethren of the children of Israel" in his epigraph. The epigraph, then, does not restrict the divine prohibition against enslavement to only the enslavement of Israelites but widens the scope of the prohibition to the entire human race. Elsewhere in his book, Cugoano provides the chapter or verse references when he combines different biblical texts into one quotation. For example, when combining Numbers 15:16 and Matthew 7:12, he writes, "One law, and one manner shall be for you, and for the stranger that sojourneth with you; and therefore, all things whatsoever ye would that men should do to you, do ye even so to them. *Numb. xv.16.—Math. vii.12.*"[12] But on the title page, he does not identify his combination of Exodus 21:16 and Deuteronomy 24:7 by chapter and verse, but simply as "LAW OF GOD" in all capital letters, as if to impress upon his readers the divine stance against slavery everywhere.[13]

On September 15, 1791, Jonathan Edwards (the younger), not to be confused with his better-known father of the same name, preached a sermon titled "The Injustice and Impolicy of the Slave Trade, and of the Slavery of the Africans" in New Haven at the annual meeting of the Connecticut branch of the Society for the Relief of Free Negroes Unlawfully Held in Bondage. Founded in Philadelphia, the organization, which became popularly known as the Pennsylvania Abolition Society, was the very first abolitionist society in the United States. In his sermon Edwards argues that "to hold a Negro slave is a greater sin than fornication, theft or robbery."[14] To support this claim, Edwards quotes Exodus 21:16 and comments, "Thus death is, by the divine express declaration, the punishment due to the crime of man-stealing. But death is not the punishment declared by God due to fornication, theft or robbery in common cases. Therefore we have the divine authority to assert, that manstealing is a greater crime than fornication, theft or robbery."[15]

A few months later, on January 29, 1792, Abraham Booth preached a sermon on Exodus 21:16 with the lengthy title, "Commerce in the Human Species, and the Enslaving of Innocent Persons, Inimical to the Laws of Moses and the Gospel of Christ." In this sermon, Booth, a Baptist minister in England who joined the Pennsylvania Abolition Society, interprets the reference to manstealers in 1 Timothy 1:10 as an example of the types of stealing prohibited by the eighth commandment. Booth proclaims, "Manstealing is here classed with such crimes as are most detestable in the sight of God, most pernicious to society, and most deserving of death by the sword of the magistrate."[16] While 1 Timothy 1:10 does not explicitly call for manstealers to be put to death, Booth finds support in Exodus 21:16 for the view that manstealers deserve to die. Like Jonathan Edwards the younger, Booth uses Exodus 21:16 to show how severe a sin slavery is in the eyes of God. While not explicitly calling for the death penalty for those involved in the slave trade on the basis of Exodus 21:16, Edwards and Booth appeal to biblical texts condemning manstealing as part of larger theological arguments that the entire slave industry is morally incompatible with biblical teachings. Booth explains that both sellers and buyers of human beings are implicated in a moral crime: "as the manstealer himself deserves to die for his flagitious crime, the purchaser of those who are become the victims of his avarice cannot be counted innocent. *Innocent*! Far from it!"[17]

Denmark Vesey, by contrast, pursued the implications of Exodus 21:16 in a more radical direction, with real-world consequences. The trials of Vesey's alleged associates continued after his death on July 2, 1822. According to Hamilton's *Account*, John Enslow gave his first confession on July 13. The evidence that he offered was "much appreciated by the Court."[18] Unlike many others implicated in the plot, John was not sentenced to die. Instead, he was to be "imprisoned in the Work House of Charleston until his Master under the direction of the City Council of Charleston shall send him out of the limits of the United States into which he is not to return under penalty of death."[19] After John's conviction, he gave a second confession detailing how Vesey planned to carry out the insurrection. He also provided information about the planning meetings. As noted in the previous chapter, he testified, "Denmark had several Meetings at different times, he generally opened them by reading the 21st Chapter of *Exodus* and exhorting them from the 16th verse; he that Stealeth a man and Selleth, or if he be found in his hands shall surely be put to death."[20] It was not uncommon for enslaved witnesses to refer to, or at least allude to, biblical texts throughout the trials. But John's quotation of Exodus 21:16 in its entirety is the only instance in any of the trial transcripts where a witness quotes a biblical text by chapter and verse when claiming that Vesey used the Bible to justify his plot. This may be because this verse was well known among antislavery advocates by the early nineteenth century.

In the end, John's confessions did not save his life. While imprisoned in the Work House awaiting his banishment, he died of an unspecified cause, despite his slaveholder Joseph Enslow's claim that "the aforementioned Slave when put under confinement was a healthy and able-bodied person."[21]

––––––

In all likelihood, Vesey would have agreed with the expelled Presbyterian clergyman Bourne and other early abolitionists' appeals to Exodus 21:16 to argue that slavery is a sin. But, unlike Bourne and other antislavery clergy, Vesey was not interested in simply making a theological argument against slavery. He saw the Bible as commanding the God-fearing to take action—to punish the perpetrators of slavery in his community. Vesey identified with the ancient Israelites of the Old Testament, and, as Kennedy and Parker note, "in all his conversations [with other people of African descent] he identified their situation with that of the Israelites."[22] For Vesey, the Bible enjoins its readers to take on the role of biblical characters and to act as they do. In other words, the Bible does not simply provide its readers with moral edification. Living biblically means enacting the Bible's laws, which requires the killing of the white slave-holding population in Charleston and the surrounding areas.

As Vesey saw it, Charleston was an example of a city facing a severe and divinely ordained punishment. His intention was to make the white proslavery clergy in Charleston admit that they had concealed texts like Exodus 21:16 from enslaved people. In her letter to her sister dated July 5, 1822, Mary Lamboll Beach acknowledges that Vesey knew that a local minister named Benjamin Palmer had met with "some of the gentlemen in our Church & made a Catechism *different* for the Negroes."[23] On the night of the insurrection, the plan was to confront some of the clergy with biblical texts like Exodus 21:16 and, as Bacchus put it in what was allegedly his fourth confession, ask them directly: "Why they did not preach up this thing?"[24] In their transcription of Bacchus's confession, Kennedy and Parker make a notation at the bottom of the page, which reads, "The Passages alluded to were Exodus 1st Chap. & 21st Chap & the 16th verse. also. 19th Chap Isiah [*sic*], and 14 Zechariah 1 & 3 verses &c."[25] Kennedy and Parker do not explain why Vesey intended to demand an explanation of Exodus 1 or Isaiah 19 from these white clergy members, but the relevance of Exodus 1 for Vesey seems clear. It tells the story of how Pharaoh enslaved the Israelites in Egypt. Although not as well known as the story in Exodus, Isaiah 19 contains a lengthy prophecy condemning Egypt and promising a severe, divinely inflicted punishment before the land of Egypt is redeemed. Kennedy and Parker explain the relevance of Zechariah 14:1–3 and Joshua 6:21 in the introduction to their *Official Report.* They claim that these two biblical texts were among Vesey's favorites. Unlike Exodus 1 and Isaiah 19, Kennedy and Parker quote the full texts of Zechariah 14:1–3 and Joshua 6:21, which they mistakenly identify as Joshua 4:21, from the King James Version. The passage from Zechariah is a prophecy about the destruction of Jerusalem in which the prophet claims that God will bring the nations against the city: "Behold, the day of the LORD cometh, and thy spoil shall be divided in the midst of thee. For I will gather all nations against Jerusalem to battle; and the city shall be taken, and the houses rifled, and the women ravished; and half of the city shall go forth into captivity, and the residue of the people shall not be cut off from the city. Then shall the LORD go forth, and fight against those nations, as when he fought in the day of battle" (Zechariah 14:1–3).

Joshua 6:21 is much shorter. It comes from the well-known story of Joshua and the Israelites' conquest of the city of Jericho upon their arrival in Canaan. After the walls famously came tumbling down, the narrator succinctly states, "And they utterly destroyed all that was in the city, both man and woman, young and old, and ox, and sheep, and ass, with the edge of the sword."[26] At first glance, the passages from Zechariah and Joshua may seem very different. Zechariah 14 is a prophecy about a future event, whereas Joshua 6 is a story about the Israelites' past. Nonetheless, there is a common denominator. Both texts address the violent fate of a city. Zechariah warns of Jerusalem's future, and Joshua recounts Jericho's past. In both texts, the inhabitants of these cities face a biblically endorsed massacre. For Vesey, Jerusalem and Jericho are examples of cities that have come under divine condemnation. And as Kennedy and Parker inform us in their notation to Bacchus Hammet's confession, Vesey included Egypt—the land of the Israelites' bondage—as another place under divine condemnation. Vesey concluded that Charleston is simply a modern-day example of this type of divinely condemned city.

Kennedy and Parker do not claim to provide an exhaustive list of all the biblical texts that Vesey may have employed to recruit others to his cause. Some biographers of Vesey have speculated about other passages that he may have used. For example, in 1999, David Robertson, who is a novelist rather than a historian, claimed that, in addition to Joshua 6:21, "Vesey had a personal fascination" with Exodus 9:1. "Then the Lord said to Moses, Go in to Pharaoh and say to him, Thus says the Lord, the God of the Hebrews, Let my people go, that they may serve me."[27] Yet, there is no evidence in any of the court documents or literature produced in the aftermath of the trials suggesting that Vesey or his associates appealed to this verse, much less had a "personal fascination" with it. (Oddly, Robertson does not mention Zechariah 14:1–3.)[28]

The process of identifying all of the texts that Vesey may have used is further complicated by the fact that the confessions and testimonies included in the *Official Report* and the other trial transcripts may allude to certain biblical texts but rarely quote these texts or provide the specific verse references for these texts. The rare exception of Exodus 21:16 notwithstanding, witnesses used common biblical idioms that could come from any number of biblical texts. For example, Rolla Bennett recounted Vesey's use of the Bible in testimony that he gave during his own trial. As discussed in the introduction, Rolla claims that he attended a meeting at Vesey's house at which Vesey "was the first to rise up and speak, and he read to us from the Bible, *how the Children of Israel were delivered out of Egypt from bondage*; he said that the rising would take place, last Sunday night week, (the 16th June)."[29] Rolla uses a common biblical idiom that describes the Israelites' liberation from slavery as God delivering them out of Egypt and out of the house of bondage. For example, Exodus 13:3 reads in part, "And Moses said unto the people, Remember this day, in which ye came out from Egypt, out of the house of bondage; for by strength of hand the LORD brought you out from this place." This idiom also occurs in Exodus 13:14 and 20:2; Deuteronomy 5:6, 6:12, 8:14, 13:5, and 13:10; Joshua 24:17; and Judges 6:8. Vesey could have read to Rolla and others gathered at the meeting from any or all of these texts that used this biblical idiom.

Apart from Kennedy and Parker's introduction in the *Official Report*, there are no direct citations of Joshua 6:21 anywhere in the trial transcripts. Kennedy and Parker may have listed this text as one of Vesey's favorite biblical verses because they assumed that it was the passage that some of the witnesses had in mind during their testimonies. For example, Jesse Blackwood allegedly confessed to Dr. Daniel Hall, a local Methodist minister who was said to have visited Vesey and his associates in jail. According to this confession, Jesse claimed that Vesey instructed those involved in plotting the insurrection to set fires to draw the white residents out in order to ambush them: "He then proceeded to explain his plan, by saying, that they intended to make the attack by setting the governor's mills on fire, and also some houses near the water, and as soon as the bells began to ring for fire, that they should kill every man as he came out of his door, and that the servants in the yard should do it, and that it should be done with axes and clubs, and afterwards they should murder the women and children, for he said, God had so commanded it in the scriptures."[30]

Similarly, after he was sentenced to death, Rolla Bennett allegedly made another confession to Hall that is strikingly similar to the confession that Jesse made to Hall.

The best way, said he, for us to conquer the whites, is to set the town on fire in several places, at the Governor's Mills, and near the Docks, and for every servant in the yards to be ready with axes and knives and clubs, to kill every man, as he came out when the bells began to ring. *He then read in the Bible where God commanded, that all should be cut off, both men, women and children, and said, he believed, it was no sin for us to do so, for the Lord had commanded us to do it.* But if I had read these Psalms, Doctor, which I have read, since I have been in this prison, they would never have got me to join them—At another meeting, some of the company were opposed to killing the Ministers, and the women and children, but Denmark said, it was not safe to keep one alive, but to destroy them totally, for you see, said he, the Lord has commanded it.[31]

Neither Jesse's nor Rolla's confessions indicate the specific biblical text that commands the murder of men, women, and children that Vesey allegedly cited. In addition to Joshua 6:21, the commands that Jesse and Rolla allude to could just as easily come from Numbers 21, Numbers 31:8–18, Deuteronomy 3:3–7, or Deuteronomy 20:16–17, among other passages. In fact, the wording of Deuteronomy 3:6—which specifically refers to "utterly destroying the men, women, and children"—is closer to the wording of Jesse's and Rolla's confessions than that of Joshua 6:21. None of the witnesses at the trials confirm that Joshua 6:21 was one of Vesey's favorite texts as Kennedy and Parker claim.

––––––––––

The only undeniable reference to Joshua 6 outside of the introductory narrative to the *Official Report* comes from an editorial by a Charleston native, attorney by training, slaveholder, and colleague of Kennedy and Parker named Benjamin Elliott.[32] Although he was not directly involved in the trials, Elliott had close associations with Kennedy and Parker.[33] His information about Vesey's biblical interpretations presumably came from those directly involved in the trials. Identifying himself only as "A South Carolinian," Elliott published a proslavery article about Vesey's plot titled "To Our Northern Brethren" in the local *City Gazette and Commercial Daily Advertiser* on September 27, 1822.[34] The article includes a reference to how "Joshua levelled the walls of Jericho."[35] But the article also suggests that the biblical texts with which Vesey engaged went well beyond those cited in the trial transcripts. Elliott's article indicates, in other words, that we should take Kennedy and Parker's references to specific biblical texts as a representative rather than exhaustive list of the texts to which Vesey appealed. At most, we can say that the passages that Kennedy and Parker reference in the *Official Report* represent the type of biblical texts used by Vesey rather than all of the texts that he used.

In addition to the direct reference to the battle of Jericho in Joshua 6, Elliott alludes to other biblical texts:

All the severe penal laws of the Israelites were quoted to mislead [Vesey's followers], and the denunciations in the prophecies, which were intended to deter men *from* evil, were declared to be divine commands which they were *to execute*. To confirm this doctrine, they were told that Heshbon, that Bashan with its sixty cities had been destroyed, man, woman and child; that in the desolation of Midian, only the males were destroyed, at which Moses was displeased, and deliberately ordered the death of the boys and their mothers. That Joshua levelled the walls of Jericho, and regarded neither age nor sex; and that David vanquished empires and left not man, woman or infant alive.[36]

Although we cannot be certain, Elliott's references to "the severe penal laws of the Israelites" may allude to Exodus 21:16, as this is the only legal punishment from the Bible that is directly referenced anywhere in the count documents. Also, "the denunciations in the prophecies" could refer to Isaiah 19 or Zechariah 14:1–3. Elliott's other biblical references are much easier to identify despite the fact that he does not cite specific chapters and verses. He describes the destruction of Heshbon and Bashan as narrated in Deuteronomy 3:3–7. In this text, Moses recalls how the Israelites killed "Og also, the king of Bashan, and all his people: and we smote him until none was left to him remaining" and "Sihon king of Heshbon, utterly destroying the men, women, and children, of every city."[37] What Elliott describes as the "desolation of Midian" refers to the Israelites' war with the Midianites in Numbers 31:7–18. After the Israelites kill all the Midianite men, Moses commands them to "kill every male among the little ones, and kill every woman that hath known man by lying with him."[38] Finally, Elliott's remark that "David vanquished empires and left not man, woman or infant alive" refers to 1 Samuel 27:8–9.[39] When we include the biblical references that Elliott cites, it appears that when Jesse Blackwood or Rolla Bennett claimed that Vesey cited texts calling for the slaughter of men, women, and children, he may have read from Numbers 31, Deuteronomy 3, or 1 Samuel 27 just as easily as Joshua 6. As mentioned in the introduction, Archibald Henry Grimké declared that Vesey "ransacked the Bible" for texts that he could use in support of his cause. It seems that Vesey's use of biblical texts was more extensive than the few passages that Kennedy and Parker mention by chapter and verse in their *Official Report*.

Elliott's article suggests that Vesey justified the slaughter of the white residents of Charleston by creating analogies involving divinely condemned locations such as Jerusalem, Jericho, or Egypt and by comparing the white residents of Charleston with the inhabitants of Canaan and other lands conquered by the Israelites. Vesey not only identified the situation of people of African descent in the United States with that of the ancient Israelites, as Kennedy and Parker claim. He also identified the white residents of Charleston with inhabitants living in and around Canaan, if what Elliott says is accurate.[40] For Vesey, the biblical stories of these conflicts provided models for how to carry out an insurrection in Charleston. To perform this insurrection biblically would require nothing less than a massacre "however shocking and bloody" as Kennedy and Parker write in their introduction, "might be the consequences."

———

In 1863, over forty years after Vesey's death, William Wells Brown wrote a profile of Vesey in his book *The Black Man: His Antecedents, His Genius, and His Achievements*. Brown was a formerly enslaved man thought to be the first African American man to publish a novel. He claimed that Vesey made antislavery arguments from the Bible during conversations with white people. "He had studied the Scriptures, and never lost an opportunity of showing that they were opposed to chattel-slavery," Brown wrote. "He spoke freely with the slaves upon the subject, and often with whites, where he found he could do so without risk to his own liberty."[41] Although Brown does not specify the texts that Vesey cited to his white interlocutors, he implies that Vesey's antislavery interpretations of the Bible were public knowledge well before the white authorities learned of his plot.

A testimony recorded in the trial transcripts corroborates Brown's claim. On June 26, 1822, Benjamin Ford, described by Kennedy and Parker as "a white Lad about 15 or 16 years of age," testified that Vesey frequented his family's shop. Vesey's "general conversation was about religion, which he would apply to Slavery," Ford reported. "[H]e would speak of the creation of the World in which he would say all men had equal rights, blacks and well as Whites &c. All his religious remarks were mingled with Slavery."[42] A confession by Bacchus Hammet gives us a sense of how Vesey would connect creation with racial equality. After Vesey got Bacchus to acknowledge that God made both Bacchus and his slaveholder, Vesey allegedly stated, "*then ar'nt you as good as your master if God made him & you, ar'nt you as free.*"[43] Ford's testimony indicates that white Charlestonians knew that Vesey used the Bible to argue for racial equality. Publically, Vesey made theological arguments against slavery by appealing to the Bible. By 1822, this was not uncommon, as evidenced by the writings of Bourne, Wesley, and other white antislavery theologians discussed earlier in this chapter.

Using the Bible to argue for racial equality in public, however, is quite different from plotting an insurrection in private. During class meetings without white people in attendance, Vesey was not simply identifying biblical texts that would help to make a scriptural case against slavery. He was identifying the biblical roles and plotlines that he exhorted his fellow conspirators to enact.[44] In public, Vesey interpreted biblical texts to make a case against slavery. In private, he planned to perform biblical roles that would strike a lethal blow against slaveholders.

CHAPTER TWO

By the Mouth of Witnesses

Whoso killeth any person, the murderer shall be put to death
by the mouth of witnesses: but one witness shall not testify
against any person to cause him to die.

—NUMBERS 35:30

On Friday June 22, 1822, the day Denmark Vesey was arrested,
the *Charleston Courier* published an essay by United States Su-
preme Court Justice William Johnson titled "Melancholy Effect
of Popular Excitement."[1] In the weeks following Vesey's execution, it was reprinted in newspapers across the nation.[2] The
essay by Johnson, a native of Charleston and a brother-in-law
of South Carolina Governor Thomas Bennett, is a cautionary
tale about the dark places to which gossip based on unfounded
rumors can take a community. In his essay, Johnson reminded
his readers of a hoax that occurred a decade or so earlier, in 1810
or 1811, when the militias of Georgia and South Carolina were
put on high alert after a letter—presumably about a revolt
against slavery—surfaced. The letter ultimately turned out to
an April Fool's Day joke, but it had deadly consequences, leading to, as Johnson put it, "a most tragical termination."[3]

Shortly after this hoax letter was released, a cavalry trumpeter stationed in Augusta, Georgia, spent the night in South Carolina en route to rejoining his company. While drinking whiskey with a companion, he thought it would be funny to blow his trumpet to see how the already-tense militia would react. Upon hearing the trumpet blast, "the detachments galloped off in all directions in quest of the offender, and towards morning returned with a single poor half-witted negro, who had been taken crossing a field on his way home, without instrument of war or of music."[4] After being whipped and threatened with death, the prisoner confessed that an enslaved blacksmith named Billy had a trumpet. Billy was promptly roused from his bed and arrested, despite a lack of motive and the fact that Billy's horn was found in a state of disuse, covered and filled with cobwebs.[5] A Court of Magistrates and Freeholders was hastily organized, and Billy was sentenced to die the next day.

In his essay, Johnson questioned the conduct of the court that convicted Billy. Since the court had received evidence that Billy had once been charged with stealing a pig, Johnson noted that "his guilt or innocence as to the pig soon took the lead of every other question on the trial." Billy's slaveholder, along with several friends, plead for "a more deliberate hearing." Yet, their pleas were to no avail as the "presiding magistrate actually conceived his dignity attacked." Johnson concludes his essay by somberly reporting that Billy was hanged "amidst crowds of execrating spectators;—and such appeared to be the popular demand for a victim, that it is not certain a pardon could have saved him."[6]

Although Johnson did not make the obvious comparison to current events in Charleston, the parallels to Vesey's arrest and the Court of Magistrates and Freeholders convened by Charleston's Mayor James Hamilton were not lost on his readers. On June 23, the day after Johnson's essay was published, Hamilton, who at the time owned multiple plantations and enslaved approximately two hundred people, wrote a short rebuttal in the Charleston *Southern Patriot, and Commercial Advertiser*.[7] Addressed "To the Public," Hamilton's response defended his court against any comparisons with what he called "the atrocious hoax at Augusta," insisting that he arranged "such a court for respectability and intelligence as has rarely been convened on any occasion in our country." He accused Johnson of unjustly libeling his fellow citizens. Despite Hamilton's best efforts, however, criticisms of his court would dog coverage of the trials of Vesey and his associates for months to come.

———

Soon after the trials concluded, local politicians sought to set the record straight about the court's procedures and the events leading up to them. Rumors had been spreading about how the court conducted its investigation. Information, or some would say misinformation, was being leaked. "It excites surprise how many things have got out when it is said the Court was under Oath to secrecy," Mary Lamboll Beach wrote in a letter to her sister Elizabeth Gilchrist dated July 25, 1822.[8] On August 13, the City Council passed a resolution that, in his capacity as Charleston's intendant, Hamilton "be requested to prepare for publication, an account of the late intended Insurrection in this City, with a Statement of the Trials and such other facts in connexion with the same as may be deemed of public interest."[9] Three days later, Hamilton completed his forty-six-page pamphlet titled *An Account of the Late Intended Insurrection among a Portion of the Blacks of the City*.

This pamphlet marked the first publication of court documents from the trials held earlier that summer. Addressing his account "to the public," Hamilton vowed transparency. In the preface, he explained that he felt "a full publication of the prominent circumstances of the late commotion" was "the most judicious course, as suppression might assume the appearance of timidity or injustice."[10] His pamphlet opens with a summary of the events that led up to the arrests of Vesey and his associates. It also provides a brief biography of Vesey—discussed in the introduction and reprinted in the appendix of this book—in a long footnote. Hamilton devoted the majority of the pamphlet, however, to summarizing the verdicts of the trials.

To assure the public that everything was done by the book, Hamilton provided his readers with the legal precedent from which the court operated. "In order that the public may understand the offence as defined in the Act of 1740," Hamilton wrote, "the clause, at length, will be found in the Appendix, marked (A.)."[11] This lengthy clause, reproduced in an appendix of Hamilton's pamphlet, comes from Article 17 of the Act for the Better Ordering and Governing of Negroes and Other Slaves in This Province, popularly known as the Negro Act of 1740. The South Carolina legislature passed this draconian law, consisting of fifty-three articles, in the wake of a rebellion led by enslaved Africans.[12] The rebellion occurred on Sunday, September 9, 1739, when an armed group marched to Stono River, about twenty miles southwest of Charleston, killing white residents in the area and burning their houses. Other enslaved persons joined the group, and their numbers reached between sixty and one hundred. Eventually, a militia caught up with them, and a battle ensued. In total, over twenty white people and at least forty Africans were killed.

Eighty-three years later, witnesses testified that one of Vesey's collaborators named Lot, who was enslaved by Alexander J. G. Forrester, called for a meeting at the Stono River when planning the insurrection.[13] Whatever symbolic significance Stono had for Vesey and his collaborators, for Hamilton the main point of Stono was that it resulted in case law that his court could apply in the trials of Vesey and his associates. The portion of Article 17 of the Negro Act of 1740, which Hamilton quotes in his Appendix A, reads as follows:

> Every Slave who shall raise, or attempt to raise an Insurrection, in this Province, or shall endeavour to delude or entice any Slave to runaway and leave the Province, every such Slave and Slaves, and his and their accomplices, aiders and abetters, shall, on conviction thereof, as aforesaid, suffer death. *Provided always*, that it shall and may be lawful, to and for the Justices who shall pronounce sentence against such Slaves, by and with the advice and consent of the Freeholders as aforesaid, if several Slaves shall receive sentence at one time, to mitigate and alter the sentence of any Slave, other than such as shall be convicted of homicide of a white person, who they shall think may deserve mercy, and may inflict such corporal punishment (other than death) on any such Slave, as they in discretion shall think fit, any thing herein contained to the contrary thereof, in any wise notwithstanding. *Provided*, that one or more of the said Slaves who shall be convicted of the crimes or offence aforesaid, where several are concerned, shall be executed for example, to deter others from offending in the like kind.[14]

In 1805, the South Carolina legislature had passed an act that in effect expanded the applicability of Article 17. The Act for the Punishment of Certain Crimes against the State of South-Carolina, ruled that not only enslaved persons but "every person or persons" involved in the planning or carrying out an insurrection would "suffer death."[15] Although Hamilton's pamphlet does not reference the 1805 act explicitly, the court may have assumed its application to Vesey's case. Kennedy and Parker quote from the 1805 act in the appendix to their *Official Report* in relation to the four men identified as "white"— William Allen, Jacob Danders, John Igneshias, and Andrew S. Rhodes—who were tried and convicted of "a Misdemeanor in inciting Slaves to Insurrection" on October 7, 1822, by Judge Elihu Hall Bay.

In late August 1822, Hamilton's quotation of Article 17 may have given his readers the impression that the trials of Vesey and his associates were open-and-shut cases. Nevertheless, Hamilton wanted to show the public that his court went above and beyond what this legal precedent demanded for a fair and reasonable trial. After pointing his readers to the law quoted in his appendix A, Hamilton insisted that the court agreed to "a variety of rules for their [the court's] government, all of them subservient to justice as well as humanity."[16] His pamphlet lists three of these rules. First, "that no slave should be tried but in the presence of his Master or his Attorney." Second, "that the testimony of one witness, unsupported by circumstances, should lead to no conviction involving capital punishment." And third, "that the statement of the party himself, should be heard in explanation of such particulars, as seemed most inculpatory."[17]

Throughout Hamilton's brief summaries of the court's activities, he returns to one of these three rules over and over again. He seems particularly concerned to show his readers that the court abided by the requirement that the accused could not be put to death on the testimony of one witness alone. His overview of the trials of Vesey and the five other men executed with him on July 2, 1822 (Rolla Bennett, Batteau Bennett, Peter Poyas, Ned Bennett, and Jesse Blackwood) illustrates Hamilton's concern. He begins with the trial of Rolla, whose confession was discussed in the previous chapter. After noting that "Jacob Axson, Esq. [was] attending as Attorney of his master [Governor Thomas Bennett Jr.]," Hamilton continues, "It was proved, that Rolla had confessed to two persons, both of whom were examined by the Court, that he belonged to the conspiracy."[18] While trying unsuccessfully to recruit one of the witnesses to join the plot, Rolla disclosed his plan to kill "his Old Buck (his master) and the Intendant," meaning Hamilton himself, on the night of the insurrection. Hamilton claims that the same witnesses acknowledged that the plan was to kill women and children as well. "On this testimony Rolla was found guilty," Hamilton soberly concludes, "and sentenced to be executed on the 2d of July."[19]

Next, Hamilton summarizes the trial of Batteau, who was also enslaved by Governor Bennett. Hamilton does not mention whether an attorney was present, but in the *Official Report*, Kennedy and Parker indicate that Jacob Axson, who would serve as a magistrate for the second Court of Magistrates and Freeholders, which was announced on August 3 and adjourned on August 8, represented Batteau.[20] As with his summary of Rolla's trial, Hamilton begins, "It was proved that Batteau confessed to two persons (both of whom were introduced as witnesses) that he belonged to the conspiracy, and made efforts to induce them to join in the rising, by representing the extent of their preparations, and the probability of their success."[21] After claiming that Batteau had multiple conversations about the plot with the two witnesses, Hamilton concludes with the refrain, "Batteau was found guilty, and sentenced to be executed on the 2d of July."[22]

A CALENDAR,

Comprising those Arrested, their owner's names, the time of their commitment, and the manner in which they were disposed of.

Class No. 1.

Comprises those prisoners who were found guilty and executed.

Prisoners Names.	Owners' Names.	Time of Commit.	How Disposed of.
Peter	James Poyas	June 18	
Ned	Gov. T. Bennet	do	Hanged on Tuesday
Rolla	do.	do	the 2d July, 1822
Batteau	do.	do	on Blake's lands,
Denmark Vesey	A free black man	22	near Charleston.
Jessy	Thos. Blackwood	23	
John	Elias Horry	July 5	Do. on the lines near
Gullah Jack	Paul Pritchard	do	Ch.; Friday July 12
Mingo	Wm. Harth	June 21	
Lot	Forrester	2↓	
Joe	P. L. Jore	July 6	
Julius	Thos. Forrest	8	
Tom	Mrs. Russell	10	
Smart	Rob't. Anderson	do.	
John	John Robertson	11	
Robert	do.	do.	
Adam	do.	do.	
Polydore	Mrs. Faber	do.	Hanged on the lines
Bacchus	Benj. Hammet	do.	near Charleston,
Dick	Wm. Sims	13	on Friday, 26th,
Pharoah	Mrs. Thompson	do.	July.
Jemmy	Mrs. Clement	18	
Jerry	Mordecai Cohen	19	
Dean	Jas. Mitchell	do.	
Jack	Mrs. Purcell	12	
Bellisle	Est. of Jos. Yates	18	
Naphur	do.	do.	
Adam	do.	do.	
Jack	John S. Glen	16	
Charles	John Billings	18	
Jack	N. McNeill	22	
Cæsar	Miss Smith	do.	Do. Tues. July 30.
Jacob Stagg	Jacob Lancaster	23	
Tom	Wm. M. Scott	24	
*William	Mrs. Garner	Aug. 2	Do. Friday Aug. 9

* Tried by the last Court.

FIGURE 3. List in Kennedy and Parker's *Official Report* of executed prisoners, including Denmark Vesey.

After briefly noting the acquittal of Stephen, who was enslaved by the wealthy plantation owner Thomas Rhett Smith, Hamilton turns to the trial of Peter, who was enslaved by James Poyas. Hamilton charged that Peter "had made great efforts to induce others to join in the insurrection; and the testimony represented him quite in the character of a chieftain or leader."[23] Hamilton does not provide the exact number of witnesses who testified against Peter, but he does indicate that there was more than one. That Peter would have been in charge of securing the Main Guard House during the insurrection "was strongly to be inferred, from *all the witnesses* stated."[24] Again, Hamilton concludes with the now familiar refrain, "Peter was found guilty on this testimony, and sentenced for execution on the 2d of July."[25] Hamilton does not indicate whether Peter's slaveholder or an attorney was present during Peter's trial, although, in the *Official Report*, Kennedy and Parker indicate that Robert Bentham served as his counsel and was in attendance.[26]

Hamilton lists several other acquittals before turning to the trial of Ned, who, like Rolla and Batteau, was enslaved by Governor Bennett. Once again, Hamilton does not mention an attorney present, but in the *Official Report*, Kennedy and Parker indicate that the governor's attorney Jacob Axson represented Ned.[27] Hamilton makes a point, however, of noting that multiple witnesses testified against Ned. "*Ned's* guilt was proved fully by the same witnesses that appeared against Peter Poyas, with whom it was established he was in the habit of frequent consultation on the efforts that were to be made."[28] Based on the testimony of these unidentified witnesses, Hamilton concludes that Ned "was found guilty, and sentenced for execution on the 2d of July."[29]

As we might expect, Hamilton saved his longest summary for the trial of Denmark Vesey. He notes that Vesey was assisted by his counsel, George W. Cross, a lawyer who at one time was

Vesey's landlord when Vesey lived on Bull Street in Charleston. Although Hamilton does not provide the exact number of witnesses who testified against Vesey, he claims that they were more than enough to convict him. Hamilton remarks, "From the testimony of most of the witnesses, however, the Court found enough, and amply enough, to warrant the sentence of death, which, on the 28th, they passed on him."[30] Hamilton goes on to explain that Vesey's house served as "the place appointed for the secret meetings of the conspirators, at which he was invariably a leading and influential member."[31] Although Hamilton does not indicate to which biblical texts Vesey appealed, he declares that Vesey encouraged others to join the plot "by the grossest prostitution and perversion of the sacred oracles."[32] Hamilton deviates slightly from his standard refrain when recording the verdict against Vesey. He directs his readers to the confessions of several enslaved men, which he quotes in the pamphlet's appendixes B, D, H, and K. "The peculiar circumstances of guilt, which confer a distinction on his case, will be found narrated in the confessions of Rolla, Monday Gell, Frank and Jesse, in the Appendix [marked B, K, D, and H, respectively]. He was sentenced for execution on the 2d July."[33] Hamilton makes it abundantly clear to his readers that Vesey was convicted on the testimony of more than one witness.

In the introductory narrative to their *Official Report*, Kennedy and Parker illustrate how, at Vesey's trial, the court supposedly followed an additional guideline that Hamilton did not include in his pamphlet. According to Kennedy and Parker, this stricture insisted that "the statements or defences of the accused should be heard, in every case, and they be permitted themselves to examine any witness they thought proper." After his counsel had cross-examined the witnesses, Kennedy and Parker report that Vesey asked to examine them himself:

He at first questioned them in the dictatorial, despotic manner, in which he was probably accustomed to address them; but this was not producing the desired effect, he questioned them with affected surprise and concern for bearing false testimony against him; still failing in his purpose, he then examined them strictly as to dates, but could not make them contradict themselves. The evidence being closed, he addressed the Court at considerable length, in which his principal endeavour was to impress them with the idea, that as his situation in life had been such that he could have had no inducement to join in such an attempt, that charge against him must be false; and he attributed it to the great hatred which he alleged the blacks had against him; but his allegations were unsupported by proof. When he received his sentence, the tears trickled down his cheeks.[34]

It is unfortunate that Kennedy and Parker provide only a summary rather than a transcript of Vesey's cross-examination and his address to the court in the *Official Report*. But, then, the goal of publishing court documents was not to allow Vesey to make his case, even in death, in the court of public opinion. Rather, the publications aimed to defend the court's actions.

Among the five other men executed the same day as Vesey, Hamilton summarizes Jesse Blackwood's trial last. Although Hamilton does not mention whether Jesse was tried in the presence of his slaveholder or an attorney, Kennedy and Parker indicate that his slaveholder was present in the *Official Report*.[35] Hamilton's very brief summary of Jesse's trial does not end with his standard refrain. Instead, Hamilton states, "The testimony against Jesse was very ample. His activity and zeal, in promoting the views of Denmark Vesey, in relation to the plot, were fully proved."[36] After an overview of Jesse's recruiting efforts, Hamilton quotes what Jesse allegedly said "to the *witnesses*" before claiming, "All the particulars in proof against him, he confirmed after receiving his sentence, by his own full and satisfactory Confession, which will be found in the Appendix, marked (H.)"[37] After summarizing the trials of what Hamilton refers to as the six "ringleaders," he reviews a number of other trials, often referring the reader to the appropriate appendixes for the evidence against the accused.[38]

———

To demonstrate that the court followed its agreed-upon guideline that required the consideration of testimony from the accused, Hamilton concludes his summary of these trials of the six alleged ringleaders by reporting, "Sentence of death was passed on these six men, on the 28th of June, and they were executed on the 2d of July. With the exception of Jesse and Rolla, they made no disclosures [meaning confessions]."[39] As to the other two guidelines for the court included in his pamphlet, Hamilton does not always confirm whether the accused were tried in the presence of their slaveholders or an attorney. But he does confirm that there were multiple witnesses against each of the accused ringleaders who were put to death. Even before Hamilton published his pamphlet, white Charlestonians took notice of the court's adherence to the guideline concerning multiple witnesses. For example, Mary Lamboll Beach wrote a letter to her sister on Friday, July 5, three days after Denmark Vesey was hanged, in which she insisted on the integrity of the trials. She observed, "They convict none on a single testimony."[40]

The legal precedent for the guideline concerning multiple witnesses was well established by the summer of 1822. A very similar rule regarding witnesses appears in Nathaniel Ward's 1641 *Massachusetts Body of Liberties*, the first set of published laws in colonial America. Among the rules listed under "Rites Rules and Liberties concerning Juditiall proceedings," number 47 states, "No man shall be put to death without the testimony of two or three witnesses or that which is equivalent thereunto."[41] Similarly, the 1805 Act for the Punishment of Certain Crimes against the State of South-Carolina, discussed earlier, states that "by confession in open court, or by the testimony of two witnesses," a person may be found "guilty of treason against the state, and suffer Death."[42]

We will never know for certain why Beach singles out this particular guideline, which would later appear in both Hamilton's *Account* and Kennedy and Parker's *Official Report*, when writing to her sister. It is possible that she knew of the legal history behind this guideline or that she genuinely believed that the rules governing the court's procedures seem to show a concern for the rights of the accused. But this guideline could also resonate with a public steeped in teachings based on texts from the Bible. The requirement for more than one witness in a capital case was known not only from the *Massachusetts Body of Liberties* and the Act for the Punishment of Certain Crimes against the State of South-Carolina. It came from biblical law, as the epigraph for this chapter from Numbers 35:30 indicates. Technically, this verse addresses those who have already committed a homicide rather than those, like Vesey, who were accused of plotting homicides. Yet, there are other biblical laws that require more than one witness for capital punishment regardless of the alleged offense. Deuteronomy 17:6 states, "At the mouth of two witnesses, or three witnesses, shall he that is worthy of death be put to death; but at the mouth of one witness he shall not be put to death." Deuteronomy 19:15 requires multiple witnesses even in cases that do not involve a capital offense or capital punishment. It states, "One witness shall not rise up against a man for any iniquity, or for any sin, in any sin that he sinneth: at the mouth of two witnesses, or at the mouth of three witnesses, shall the matter be established."

To be clear, Hamilton does not explicitly cite these biblical laws about the required number of witnesses anywhere in his pamphlet. In fact, unlike the rest of the pamphlets discussed in this book, Hamilton's *Account* does not explicitly allude to or quote any biblical texts, except when they appear in the quoted statements from other sources. For example, Hamilton quotes from a brief letter that was allegedly found among the belongings of Abraham, who was enslaved by Dr. John Earnest Poyas Jr. The letter, which seems to refer to Vesey's plot, includes the line, "Fear not, the Lord God that delivered Daniel is able to deliver us." Most likely, this is a reference to the popular biblical story of God's deliverance of Daniel from the lions' den (Daniel 6:27).[43] Hamilton, however, does not comment on this biblical reference. Also, in the last two of pages of the pamphlet, Hamilton quotes two of the death sentences handed down by Lionel Henry Kennedy on July 9, a week after Vesey was hanged.[44] The first sentence condemned Jack Pritchard, commonly known as Gullah Jack. During Jack's sentence, Kennedy quotes from Luke 3:7 and Ecclesiastes 9:10. Kennedy's second sentence condemned ten other enslaved persons— Charles Billings, Jemmy Clement, Jerry Cohen, Bacchus Hammet, Dean Mitchell, William Paul, Adam Robertson, Dick Sims, Bellisle Yates, and Naphur Yates—to death.[45] As part of this sentence, Kennedy quotes Proverbs 3:17 and Ephesians 6:5–6, and alludes to Genesis 3:19 and Genesis 9:20–27. I discuss Kennedy's use of biblical texts when delivering his verdicts against Vesey and his associates in the next chapter. But the point for now is that Hamilton does not comment on Kennedy's biblical references or make any of his own.

Nevertheless, to claim biblical authority in the antebellum South was not just a matter of citing biblical texts directly in order to justify one's actions or beliefs. In a culture that understood the Bible as authoritative, one could claim authority for oneself by enacting roles that would be publicly recognizable as biblical, especially in cases when one's authority would otherwise be challenged, dismissed, or unrecognized. In Vesey's case, this meant that his identification of people of African descent with ancient Israelites would become recognizably biblical through an insurrection that resembled the Israelites' conquest of Canaan.[46] For Hamilton, the court that he organized would become recognizably biblical—and thus more authoritative—through the biblical-sounding guidelines that it established for itself. As previously mentioned, there were challenges to the court's methods and its authority. In fact, some even questioned Hamilton's piety. In a letter dated July 25, 1822, Mary Lamboll Beach acerbically referred to him as "the young man Hamilton our Intendant who knows not God."[17]

While Article 17 of the Negro Act of 1740 may provide a legal precedent for convicting those accused of participating in Vesey's plot, the additional guidelines suggested to the public that the court was acting in accordance with a higher standard. Rather than citing selected biblical texts as endorsements of the court's conduct, Hamilton's pamphlet showed how the court enacted commands within certain biblical texts. When interpreted against the backdrop of biblical law, the public could read Hamilton's pamphlet as a labored defense of the court as if it were a biblical institution in and of itself.

CHAPTER THREE

With Fear and Trembling

Servants, be obedient to them that are your masters according
to the flesh, with fear and trembling, in singleness of your
heart, as unto Christ.

—EPHESIANS 6:5

"Why, pa," Lionel Kennedy's son exclaimed, "Payne is playing
hell in Charleston."[1] Daniel Payne had started a school for
children of African descent in 1829, seven years after Vesey's
death. At its height, the school enrolled about sixty students.
Decades after Payne was forced to shutter his school, he recounted in his memoir how three of his young students had a
run-in with Lionel Kennedy and his son. As the story goes,
Payne needed a rattlesnake for his zoological studies, so he arranged to buy one from one of the Kennedys' enslaved men on
a summer day in 1834. Payne sent his students John Lee, Robert
Wishan, and Michael Eggert to the Kennedy plantation to pick
up the snake. When they arrived at the plantation, they were
confronted by the Kennedys. Lionel and his son quizzed them,
and when the students were able to answer all but one of their
questions, the Kennedys realized that Payne was providing a

quality education to children of African descent. In their minds, Payne was playing hell in Charleston.

Payne believed that this encounter was the beginning of the end for his school and his life in Charleston. Just a few months after this incident, in December 1834, two lawyers from Charleston introduced a bill to the South Carolina legislature mandating a fine of up to fifty dollars, a beating of up to fifty lashes, and imprisonment up to six months for any free person of color or enslaved person who "keep[s] any school or other place of instruction for teaching any slave or free person of color to read or write."[2] Payne's school closed on March 31, 1835, and the law went into effect the next day. That May, Payne left Charleston for Philadelphia. He eventually became the sixth bishop of the African Methodist Episcopal Church. Although Payne does not identify by name the two lawyers responsible for the bill that drove him out of Charleston, he implies that Kennedy influenced the introduction of the bill following his encounter with Payne's pupils. Learning to read in early-nineteenth-century America meant learning to read the Bible, and Kennedy was greatly concerned about people of African descent reading the Bible outside of the supervision of white authorities. After all, twelve years earlier Kennedy had seen hell break loose in Charleston when Vesey had instructed other people of African descent on how to interpret the Bible.

———

By all accounts, Lionel Henry Kennedy was well respected by his peers. Today, by contrast, few people would know his name were it not for his association with Denmark Vesey. Without this association, his career as a lawyer and local politician at best would have merited an obscure footnote in the history of Charleston,

South Carolina. Even in his own day he would have been over-shadowed by his father James Kennedy—a native of Pennsylvania and a veteran of the Revolutionary War who served in Washington's Continental Army—were it not for Vesey's plot.

As a young man, Lionel Kennedy went north to attend Yale before returning to Charleston to practice law.[3] He then began his career in elected office, serving the same parishes that his father had represented in the South Carolina legislature. During the younger Kennedy's time at Yale, Timothy Dwight set the theological tone as the school's president and professor of divinity. Dwight was the grandson of the famed Jonathan Edwards (the elder), still considered by many today to be one of the most influential theologians in American history. Edwards himself had attended and then taught at Yale in the early eighteenth century. It is very likely that Kennedy would have encountered Edwards's ideas during his time at Yale.

The influence of Edwards's writings on Lionel Kennedy is apparent when Kennedy delivered the court's verdict against Jack Pritchard, known as Gullah Jack, on July 9, 1822. While sentencing Jack to death, Kennedy implores him to repent. "Let me then, conjure you to devote the remnant of your miserable existence, in fleeing from the '*wrath to come.*'"[4] At first glance, the italicized phrase "wrath to come" seems to come from a searing speech that stresses the importance of repentance attributed to John the Baptist in Luke 3:7–8 ("O generation of vipers, who hath warned you to flee from the wrath to come? Bring forth therefore fruits worthy of repentance").[5] Yet Kennedy is likely to have become familiar with this phrase because of its appearance in the conclusion to Edwards's best-known sermon, "Sinners in the Hands of an Angry God," delivered throughout New England in 1741. At the height of the Great Awakening, Edwards sought to impress upon New England congregations the gravity of their sinful condition. The idea that sinners can turn to God alone for mercy is a central tenet of this sermon. "Therefore let every one that is out of Christ, now awake and fly from the Wrath to come," Edwards warned at his sermon's conclusion. "The Wrath of almighty GOD is now undoubtedly hanging over [a] great Part of this Congregation."[6] Over eighty years later, Kennedy would use similar rhetoric when calling for Jack to repent.

At that same time, Kennedy's verdict against Jack dismisses traditional African medical and religious practices as mere superstition. Although Kennedy and Parker list Jack among the members of the African Church in their introductory narrative to the *Official Report*, they also claim that "vast numbers of the Africans firmly believed that Gullah Jack was a sorcerer; that he could neither be killed nor taken; and that whilst they retained the charms which he had distributed they would themselves be invulnerable."[7] But what Kennedy and Parker describe as sorcery, some witnesses described as traditional African medical and religious practices.[8] Harry Haig, who was enslaved by a Scottish immigrant named David Haig, testified, "Gullah Jack calls himself a negro doctor." He claimed that Jack "charmed" him and he "then consented to join" the plot.[9] Similarly, George Vanderhorst, who was enslaved by Richard Withers Vanderhorst, claimed that Jack "had charms."[10] Yorrick Cross described some of the materials that Jack allegedly used. Yorrick claimed that "Jack gave me some dry food, consisting of parched corn and ground nuts, and said, eat that, and nothing else, on the morning when it breaks out, and when you join us as we pass, put into your mouth this crab claw, and you can't be wounded [during the insurrection]."[11]

Although Kennedy knew Jack was a member of the African Church, he depicts Jack's practices as rooted in superstitions inferior to Christianity or, possibly, in a superstitious version of Christianity inferior to the type of Christianity that Kennedy practiced. When sentencing Jack to death, Kennedy admonishes him for enlisting "the most disgusting mummery and superstition." Kennedy concludes, "all the Powers of Darkness cannot rescue you from your approaching Fate!"[12] He exclaims, "Your boasted Charms have not preserved yourself, and of course could not protect others" because what Jack conjured has been "chased away by the superior light of Truth."[13] Since he does not recognize Jack's practices as a legitimate expression of Christianity, Kennedy encourages Jack to clear his conscience by confessing to a Christian minister of his choice. "The Court are willing to afford you all the aid in their power, and to permit any Minister of the Gospel, whom you may select to have free access to you," Kennedy informed Jack. "To him you may unburthen your guilty conscience. Neglect not the opportunity, for there is 'no device nor art in the grave,' to which you must shortly be consigned."[14] The line "no device nor art in the grave" is a very close but not exact quotation of Ecclesiastes 9:10 ("Whatsoever thy hand findeth to do, do it with thy might; for there is no work, nor device, nor knowledge, nor wisdom, in the grave, whither thou goest"). Kennedy insists that the grave will not allow Jack any opportunity to save his soul. When sentencing Jack, Kennedy appeals to the Bible as an authoritative text in Christianity to suggest that the religious expression that can save Jack is not found in the use of charms but in the unburdening of his conscience to a Christian minister.

Kennedy's verdicts in the trials related to Vesey's plot were not the first time that he used authoritative texts to bolster his arguments. He used a similar rhetorical technique in an oration that he delivered nine years earlier. This oration sheds important light on Kennedy's style of argumentation and his ap-

proach to biblical interpretation when he delivered the court's
verdicts against Vesey and his associates.

————

Founded in May 1783, the Society of the Cincinnati was a selective hereditary organization that limited its membership to
military officers who fought in the Revolutionary War and their
descendants. It soon had chapters in several states. As a veteran,
Lionel's father, James Kennedy, was elected as assistant trea-
surer at the first meeting of the society's South Carolina chapter
on August 29, 1783.[15] Each year, the South Carolina chapter
commissioned a July 4 oration commemorating the nation's independence. On July 4, 1801, James Kennedy delivered this
prestigious speech at Saint Philip's Church in Charleston.[16]
Since Lionel Kennedy was the son of an officer in the Continental Army, the society admitted him as an honorary member
on July 4, 1808.[17] Five years later, an article in the February 24,
1813, edition of Charleston's *City Gazette and Commercial Daily
Advertiser* announced that the society invited him to deliver
that year's July 4 oration, just as his father had done twelve years
earlier.[18] The local Charleston publisher W. P. Young subsequently printed Kennedy's twenty-two-page oration at the request of the South Carolina Society of the Cincinnati and the
American Revolution Society.[19]

Throughout his address, Lionel Kennedy marks several short
lines as quotations but does not include any identification of
their sources. Some come from the Bible. For example, the
opening paragraph includes a lush description of America, describing it as a "land of promise" and as a "city of refuge."[20] The
exact phrase "land of promise" comes from Hebrews 11:8–9. It
occurs nowhere else in the King James Version. The term "city

of refuge" occurs several times in the Bible, mostly in Numbers 35 and Joshua 21.[21] Several of the other unidentified quotations come from literature outside the Bible that concerns liberty. Kennedy quotes lines from early American political leaders such as Congressional Representative Fisher Ames's 1800 eulogy for George Washington before the Massachusetts state legislature and from the future governor of Virginia John Page's letter to Thomas Jefferson, dated July 20, 1776, praising Jefferson for the Declaration of Independence.[22] Kennedy also cites European authors in order to stress that liberty is not just an American ideal but a fundamental human principle. He quotes British poetry, such as Richard Glover's 1737 epic poem *Leonidas*, which praises the virtues of liberty, and Thomas Gray's 1751 masterpiece, "Elegy Written in a Country Churchyard." He also lifts lines from prominent Irish trial lawyer John Philpot Curran's statements during his defense of Archibald Hamilton Rowan, an outspoken advocate for Ireland's independence from England at Rowan's 1794 trial for "seditious libel."[23]

The dense network of quotations in this 1813 oration reveals Kennedy's predilection for quoting biblical and classical literature without identifying his sources. We find the same pattern in his ruling against Vesey. Along with the biblical references, his Vesey ruling features quotations from the English romantic poet Percy Bysshe Shelley and from William Penn in the following passage addressed directly to the accused: "Your 'lamp of life' is nearly extinguished; your race is run; and you must shortly pass 'from time to eternity.'"[24] When Kennedy sentences ten enslaved persons accused of involvement in Vesey's plot, he refers to Aesop's fable of the frozen serpent who shows ingratitude by biting and killing a man who sheltered it from the cold.[25]

When sentencing Vesey, Kennedy accused him of being "totally insensible of the divine influence of that Gospel, 'all whose paths are peace.'"[26] The "Gospel" that Kennedy quotes does not come from the New Testament Gospels—Matthew, Mark, Luke, and John—but from Proverbs 3:17: "Her ways are ways of pleasantness, and all her paths are peace." In its biblical context, this verse describes the positive qualities of wisdom, personified as a woman. Kennedy, however, quotes the verse as "all whose paths are peace" rather than "all her paths are peace." This slight modification is likely inspired by a line in the very popular English poet William Cowper's antislavery poem "Charity," published in 1782: "The paths of wisdom, all whose paths are peace."[27] It would be somewhat ironic if Kennedy's verdict against the alleged leader of an intended revolt against slaveholders incorporated a line from an antislavery poem.

Kennedy weaves together short quotations from different parts of the Bible to remind Vesey that while his earthly fate may be sealed, his soul still hangs in the balance. This lends a sense of biblical authority to the call for repentance with which he ends his delivery of the court's verdict against Vesey:

Your situation is deplorable, but not destitute of spiritual consolation. To that Almighty Being alone, whose Holy Ordinances, you have trampled in the dust, can you now look for mercy, and although "your sins be as scarlet," the tears of sincere penitence may obtain forgiveness at the "Throne of Grace." You cannot have forgotten the history of the malefactor on the Cross, who, like yourself, was the wretched and deluded victim of offended justice. His conscience was awakened in the pangs of dissolution, and yet there is reason to believe, that his spirit was received into the realms of bliss.

May you imitate his example, and may your last moments prove like his!²⁸

The line "your sins be as scarlet" comes from Isaiah 1:18, which reads "though your sins be as scarlet, they shall be as white as snow." The only use of the term "Throne of Grace" in the King James Version occurs in Hebrews 4:16, which describes the throne as the place to obtain divine mercy: "Let us therefore come boldly unto the throne of grace, that we may obtain mercy, and find grace to help in time of need." Kennedy concludes his verdict by reminding Vesey of the story in Luke 23:40–43 of the man who was crucified with Jesus but acknowledged his guilt and asked Jesus to remember him in his kingdom. For Kennedy, the story serves as a powerful example of how sinners may seek God's mercy even as their execution for their earthly crimes approaches. At first, Kennedy's use of allusions and short quotations from the Bible creates the effect that his verdict is in keeping with a divinely inspired urgent call for repentance. Yet Kennedy also appeals to the Bible in his verdict to defend slavery as a divinely ordained institution.

————

In delivering the court's verdict against Vesey, Kennedy quotes the Bible not just to stress the urgency of repentance but also to defend slavery. On the surface, several of the biblical texts that he cites may not seem to offer a full-throated endorsement of slavery. In such instances, Kennedy provides a brief commentary on the cited verses to show that they provide a justification for Charleston's slaveholding status quo. For example, in its biblical context, Proverbs 3:17 has nothing to do with slavery. Yet, immediately after declaring Vesey "totally insensible of the

divine influence of that Gospel, 'all whose paths are peace,'"
Kennedy explains the purpose of Proverbs 3:17. "It was to reconcile us to our destinies on earth," he declares, "and to enable
us to discharge with fidelity, all the duties of life, that those holy
precepts were imparted by Heaven to fallen man." A few days
later, when sentencing ten enslaved persons collectively, Kennedy returns to Proverbs 3:17 and repeats his commentary on
this verse nearly word for word. Sardonically, he asks the defendants, "Are you incapable of the Heavenly influence of that Gospel, all whose 'paths are peace?' It was to reconcile us to our
destiny on earth, and to enable us to discharge with fidelity all
our duties, whether as master or servant, that those inspired
precepts were imparted by Heaven to fallen man."[29] In other
words, for a fallen humanity to achieve the peaceful paths within
a divinely intended social structure, each person must accept her
or his earthly destiny and carry out the duties appropriate to her
or his station. This, in a nutshell, represents the essence of what
the Bible teaches humanity according to Kennedy.

Kennedy traces God's decrees for a fallen humanity back to
God's confrontation with Adam and Eve after they ate fruit
from the prohibited tree of the knowledge of good and evil in
the Garden of Eden. In Genesis 3:19, God declares to Adam, "In
the sweat of thy face shalt thou eat bread." While Kennedy does
not quote Genesis 3:19 directly, he clearly alludes to it when
sentencing the ten men collectively. As he did with Proverbs
3:17, he offers a brief commentary on this verse to show how it
applies to the present day:

That we should all earn our bread by the sweat of our brow,
is the decree which God pronounced at the fall of man. It
extended alike to the master and the slave; to the cottage and
the throne. Every one is more or less subject to controul; and

the most exalted, as well as the humblest individual, must bow with defference to the laws of that community, in which he is placed by Providence. Your situation, therefore, was neither extraordinary nor unnatural. Servitude has existed under various forms, from the deludge to the present time, and in no age or country has the condition of slaves been milder or more humane than your own.[30]

Kennedy explains that after the Fall all humans must work for their food regardless of whether they are "the master or the slave" or whether they occupy "the cottage or the throne." God decreed that all humanity will be under varying degrees of social control. Each must respect the position within the community "in which he is placed by Providence." The laws of the community reflect a divinely sanctioned order. Thus, Kennedy reasons, it is part of the natural order outside of Eden that some people would be enslaved. He insists that this social ordering is not unnatural because it comes from a divine decree. As Kennedy informs the ten enslaved men, "Your situation, therefore, was neither extraordinary nor unnatural." Genesis 3:19, for Kennedy, reveals that a social structure that includes human labor—and thus accommodates slavery—was put in place by divine decree at the Fall. Vesey's plot, then, would present a blatant violation of the natural order of things.

One could object that Genesis does not connect slavery with the Fall when God expelled Adam and Eve from Eden. A popular "origins story" for slavery in the nineteenth century does not trace its roots back to the Fall but to an odd episode involving Noah and his sons after they survive the flood (Genesis 9:25–27). In this story—which I discuss further in chapter 6—Noah curses one of his grandsons with slavery, at least according to some interpretations.[31] Kennedy makes a passing reference to this idea that the practice of slavery began only after the flood when he states, "Servitude has existed under various forms, from the deludge to the present time."[32] Nonetheless, his interpretation of Genesis 3:19 incorporates slavery into his understanding of the social structure that God decreed well before the flood, even if slavery was not practiced until after this disaster occurred.

Kennedy was not the first to use Genesis 3:19 in a proslavery context. Two years before Vesey's trial, Daniel Raymond, an influential political economist from Baltimore, interpreted the enslavement of people of African descent as a divine curse for violating the decree in Genesis 3:19, which he understood as applicable to the vast majority of humanity regardless of race. He writes in his book *Thoughts on Political Economy* in 1820:

> The great mass of mankind in all ages and in all countries have been obligated to submit to their doom of "eating bread by the sweat of their faces." And among those who have endeavored to extricate themselves from this necessity, by fraud and violence, by far the greater portion, have utterly failed, and subjected themselves to a tenfold greater curse. He who made the law [God] does not lack the ability to carry it into execution, nor does he permit it to be violated with impunity. How forcibly is this exemplified in the case of the negro slave.[33]

When read closely, however, nothing in Genesis 3:19 remotely suggests that the verse has anything to do with chattel slavery. The same may be said about the reference to the peaceful paths in Proverbs 3:17. Thus, Kennedy had to offer his brief commentaries on these verses to twist them into biblical justifications for Charleston's slaveholding status quo. Without Kennedy's rather strained commentary, how these Old Testament

AN

OFFICIAL REPORT

OF THE

TRIALS OF SUNDRY NEGROES,

CHARGED

WITH AN ATTEMPT TO RAISE

AN INSURRECTION

IN THE STATE OF SOUTH-CAROLINA:

PRECEDED BY AN

INTRODUCTION AND NARRATIVE;

AND

IN AN APPENDIX,

A REPORT OF THE TRIALS OF

FOUR WHITE PERSONS,

ON INDICTMENTS FOR ATTEMPTING TO EXCITE THE SLAVES TO
INSURRECTION.

Prepared and Published at the request of the Court.

━━⊷⊶⊷━━

By LIONEL H. KENNEDY & THOMAS PARKER,

Members of the Charleston Bar, and the Presiding Magistrates of the Court.

━━━━◗◦◗◦◗◦━━━━

CHARLESTON:

PRINTED BY JAMES R. SCHENCK, 23, BROAD-STREET.

1822.

FIGURE 4. Title page of Kennedy and Parker's *Official Report*.

texts relate to slavery in Charleston in the early nineteenth century would be entirely unclear. This differs dramatically from the texts that Kennedy quotes from the New Testament Epistles, which, as I discuss in upcoming chapters, were often cited in antebellum defenses of slavery. Unlike Genesis 3:19 or Proverbs 3:17, Kennedy believed these New Testament texts are so straightforward in their endorsement of slavery that he declared, "On such texts comment is unnecessary."[34]

In Kennedy's mind, certain biblical texts need some explanation to show how they endorse a system of slavery, while others re quire no further commentary to show their endorsement. In his verdicts against Vesey and other accused conspirators, Kennedy makes it clear that the New Testament Epistles endorse the practice of slavery and that the matter is so clear as to be self-evident. Had Vesey honestly been interested in what the Bible says about slavery, Kennedy contends, he would have been guided by the instructions found in Colossians 3:22 and 1 Peter 2:18:

> If you had searched them [the biblical texts] with sincerity, you would have discovered instructions, immediately applicable to the deluded victims of your artful wiles—"*Servants (says Saint Paul) obey in all things your masters, according to the flesh, not with eye-service, as men-pleasers, but in singleness of heart, fearing God." And again "Servants (says Saint Peter) 'be subject to your masters' with all fear, not only to the good and gentle, but also to the forward."* On such texts comment is unnecessary.[35]

Kennedy can claim that these texts need no commentary because they fit with his understanding of the need to accept one's station as revealed by God. Colossians 3:22 and 1 Peter 2:18

are not simply texts from antiquity but divine "instructions" that are "immediately applicable" to those enslaved people whom Vesey had recruited for his insurrection. Similarly, when sentencing the ten enslaved persons, Kennedy quotes Ephesians 6:5–6—which serves as the epigraph for this chapter—in its entirety. Kennedy charges that the defendants did not study the Bible "in a spirit of truth" and did not listen "with sincerity to such doctrines":

> There is no condition of life which is not embraced by them [biblical texts]; and if you had searched them, *in the spirit of truth*, you would have discovered instructions peculiarly applicable to yourselves—"*Servants (says St. Paul) be obedient to them that are your masters according to the flesh, with fear and trembling, in singleness of your heart, as unto Christ; not with eye-service as men pleasers, but as the servants of Christ, doing the will of God from the heart.*" Had you listened with sincerity to such doctrines, you would not have been arrested by an ignominious death.[36]

If the Bible deals with every "condition in life," the relationship of the enslaved and the slaveholder, Kennedy concludes, is the particular condition that Ephesians 6:5–6 addresses. The obedience of the enslaved to their slaveholders demonstrates that they are "doing the will of God from the heart." As he did at Vesey's trial, Kennedy admonishes the ten enslaved persons that these biblical texts serve as "instructions peculiarly applicable to yourselves" without the need for further elaboration or commentary.

Kennedy's assertion that texts from the Epistles are so straightforward that they need no explanation obscures the fact that he is incorporating them into his own interpretive framework based on a far-from-obvious reading of Old Testament texts as divine endorsements of slavery. What Kennedy finds truly appalling about Vesey's plot is that it went beyond treason against the state and directly attacked this tendentious framework. Kennedy declared that Vesey's "professed design was to trample on all laws, human and divine." The dense network of biblical quotations that Kennedy strings together when sentencing Vesey is meant as a defense of the framework, a reassertion that proslavery laws of the state are aligned with the laws of God. Kennedy viewed Vesey's use of the Bible as criminal because he thought Vesey read the Bible in a way that would disrupt the divinely decreed social structure rather than reconcile himself to it.

In his 1972 biography of Vesey written for young adults, John Oliver Killens wonders what went through Vesey's mind as he stood in the courtroom listening to Kennedy accuse him of perverting biblical texts in support of his plot. Killens imagines that, at that moment, "a sad smile moved across his face as he thought grimly that yes, he really had tortured the words of the Holy Book from the point of view of these 'holy' men who looked down upon him from their lofty positions at the bar of justice. Yes, he had 'perverted' the Word of God and had read in it a mandate to him to liberate his people. . . . It was a question of interpretation. And the master and the slave would never have identical interpretations."[37]

CHAPTER FOUR

Now Profitable

Which in time past was to thee unprofitable, but now
profitable to thee and to me.

—PHILEMON 11

Over the course of several letters to her sister Elizabeth Gilchrist in the summer of 1822, Mary Lamboll Beach detailed the
reaction of several white Charlestonians to the revelation of
Vesey's plot.[1] In her July 5 letter, she informed her sister that the
clergymen Artemas Boies, Richard Furman, and Benjamin
Morgan Palmer had visited Denmark Vesey and the other alleged ringleaders of the plot—Rolla Bennett, Batteau Bennett,
Ned Bennett, Peter Poyas, and Jesse Blackwood—in jail shortly
before they were all executed on July 2. Boies was the pastor of
Charleston's Second Presbyterian Church, to which Vesey was
admitted as a member in April 1817. Furman was a prominent
Baptist minister who is the focus of the next chapter. Palmer
was the minister of a congregational church known as the Circular Church at which Beach's father, John Thomas, was a former pastor.

FIGURE 5. The Circular Congregational Church
(sometime between 1861 and 1864).

Two years earlier, in 1820, Palmer and Boies were among
thirty-two white signatories supporting a petition to the South
Carolina House of Representatives put forward by twenty-six
free persons of color to open a newly erected house of worship
called the African Methodist Church. (None of the petitioners
were implicated in Vesey's plot two years later.)[2] Toward the
end of their written appeal, the petitioners insist that they did
not have "any other wish or design, than to worship the om-
nipotent ruler of the Universe 'in spirit, and in truth.'" The quotation "in spirit, and in truth" comes from John 4:23–24, in
which Jesus describes the nature of true worshippers of God.
"But the hour cometh, and now is, when the true worshippers

shall worship the Father in spirit and in truth: for the Father seeketh such to worship him. God is a Spirit: and they that worship him must worship him in spirit and in truth." By invoking this passage to describe their motives for opening their church, the petitioners present their request as in keeping with a biblically mandated form of worship. Free from any nefarious design, their sole purpose was to worship God in spirit and in truth just as Jesus commanded.

Two year later, in the wake of the failed conspiracy, Palmer would return to the Gospel of John when reconsidering whether certain professed Christians among the free persons of color in Charleston had motives other than true worship. He invoked Jesus's words from John 15:22 ("but now they have no cloak for their sin") to condemn those who profess religion "merely 'as a cloak for sin.'" The conduct of these "designing hypocrites" Palmer warned, "will correspond with their *real*, not their *assumed* character."[3]

Benjamin Morgan Palmer should not be confused with his better-known nephew of the same name who, decades later, served as a moderator for the Presbyterian Church in the Confederate States of America beginning in 1861. The elder Palmer was the fourth of sixteen children born to a slaveholder named Job Palmer and the grandson of the Reverend Samuel Palmer, who was the pastor of the Circular Church for forty years.[4] Benjamin Palmer graduated from Princeton, then the College of New Jersey, in 1800, and obtained a master's degree from the same school in 1804.[5] Later, he served as vice president of the Charleston Bible Society, an organization founded in 1810 to distribute free Bibles. As a minister at the Circular Church,

Benjamin Palmer was known for his outreach to the enslaved well before white Charlestonians learned of Vesey's plot. Rolla Bennett, one of the five men executed along with Vesey, and George Wilson, the enslaved man who revealed the plot to his slaveholder, Major John Wilson, were members of Palmer's congregation. Palmer would regularly take part in services held by and for his congregants of African descent.[6] During a visit to Charleston in the fall of 1818, Abiel Abbott, a Harvard-educated Unitarian minister from Andover, Massachusetts, mentioned Palmer's involvement with these services in a journal entry dated November 22: "I am informed by Dr. P. [Palmer] that the negroes in his congregation hold regular religious meetings where the performances are entirely by themselves & in a style perfectly astonishing as to the degree of excellence. Their music is sustained in the four parts & they perform some pieces of much taste & difficulty. The Dr. often attends these meetings to give them countenance, as a certain number of whites must be present to answer the demand of the law."[7]

Palmer was also in the habit of visiting condemned prisoners on the night before their executions. At the trials of those accused of participating in Vesey's plot, Lionel Henry Kennedy offered the condemned men the opportunity to repent when sentencing them to death, as discussed in the previous chapter. Palmer and other ministers went to the jail ostensibly to ensure that Vesey and the other alleged ringleaders had the opportunity to unburden themselves.

Two of the imprisoned men, Rolla Bennett and Jesse Blackwood, had already confessed to their involvement in the plot during their trials.[8] In her July 5 letter to her sister, Mary Lamboll Beach wrote that Rolla had been a member of Palmer's congregation for two years and that "Palmer said he appeared to be more cut down when he spoke to him of his sin."[9] She also

FIGURE 6. Old Charleston jail (present day).

reported that Jesse had "a great openness & candour in his manner & he shewed a very tender & penitent spirit."[10] There is no
evidence, by contrast, that Palmer and his fellow ministers got
Vesey or the other condemned men to repent. Beach's letter
does not mention Batteau Bennett or Ned Bennett, and none
of the trial transcripts include a confession by either of them.
Beach claimed that she heard "Vesey was in a very hardened
state in the Jail" and that Peter Poyas was "a very hardened villain" and a man who "died in a dreadful state of mind."[11] She
wrote further that when Palmer and the other ministers came
to the jail, "Vesey & Poyas's fellow would hear *nothing* they had
to say; they said they were condemned already & it was of no
use to say any thing more."[12] Similarly, Charleston's mayor,
James Hamilton, reported, "With the exception of Jesse and
Rolla, they made no disclosures."[13]

Fifteen years would pass before Palmer would reveal what
was said by any of the prisoners who refused to repent. In a

small paragraph at the bottom of the first page of the August 23, 1837, edition of the *Liberator*, a Boston-based abolitionist newspaper, Palmer is said to have related the story of "a pious black, who was forward in plotting an insurrection against the whites and was detected and sentenced to death." The article provides no further identification of this man, although context suggests that he was one of the condemned prisoners Palmer visited in 1822. Palmer explains that when the man was urged to "repent of this great sin," the man allegedly replied, "What sin? You applaud the leaders of the American Revolution, who resisted a small tax on tea; and rather than pay it killed tens of thousands, but what was that tax to our sufferings? Washington was a white man and you idolized him; but I, alas am a black man, and you hang me for the very act you applauded in him."[14] The sentiments expressed by this unidentified man who refused to call the insurrection plot a sin are consistent with the dispositions of Denmark Vesey and Peter Poyas as they faced death.

Throughout the summer of 1822, Palmer attempted to unearth the root causes that led to Vesey's plot. Like Vesey, he identified Charleston with Jerusalem, and both men used prophecies from the book of Zephaniah that condemned the inhabitants of Jerusalem. In a letter dated July 25, Beach informed her sister that within "a few weeks or short number of months at farthest [Palmer had] preached from these words 'I will search Jerusalem with Candles.'" Her comment indicates that a few weeks before Vesey was executed, Palmer preached a sermon on Zephaniah 1:12, which reads, "And it shall come to pass at that time, that I will search Jerusalem with candles, and punish the men that are settled on their lees: that say in their heart, The

LORD will not do good, neither will he do evil." Although no copies of this sermon survive, we may easily surmise its intent. Beach explained to her sister that Palmer "often used those words in prayer since that *our* Jerusalem may be searched; & indeed the search seems now begun."[15] A later sermon, given two months after Vesey's execution, on September 22, 1822, indicates what Palmer thought such scrutiny might entail.

In the sermon in question, titled "Religion Profitable: With a Special Reference to the Case of Servants," Palmer never refers to Vesey by name. As if to erase his name from the memory of his fellow white Charlestonians, he refers only to "the late iniquitous and murderous plot."[16] The publishers explain in a preface that on Sunday, September 22, the sermon was "delivered in the ordinary course of the Author's ministration among his own people." Although Palmer did not intend the sermon for publication, the publishers felt the sermon "would be generally *useful, especially in the present condition of this community; the author has concluded to give it, with a few slight alterations and some additions, a wider circulation than he intended when he wrote it*" (emphasis in the original). They believed that Palmer's biblically informed analysis of Charleston's current culture and what, in his mind, went wrong would provide comfort to a shaken community of white Charlestonians. A few months earlier, Beach's July 5 letter provided hints at how the revelation of Vesey's plot had unsettled them. She wrote that a local woman named Mary Jones "never went through such a night of Terror as that of the 16th of June . . . she said in a most solemn tone *Oh!* I shall never be able to bear the sight of a Negroe again."[17] The introductory narrative to the *Official Report* alludes to such fears when Kennedy and Parker describe their reasons for publishing their edition of the trial transcripts: "The court was likewise anxious to prevent the public mind from being excited by the exaggerated representations of the testimony which might have been circulated by auditors under the influence of misapprehension or terror."[18]

As the title of Palmer's sermon suggests, he believed that religion (that is, Christianity) is a social good that improves a person regardless of social class or civil status. "The religion of Jesus Christ," he proclaimed, "renders men profitable in every station and relation in life."[19] Unlike Vesey, who fomented his insurrection plot, in part, by using the Bible to challenge the status quo of Charleston's society, Palmer used this sermon to equate "profitable" relations between people with a defense of current social hierarchies.

For Palmer's paradigmatic example of a profitable relationship he turned to the New Testament Epistles of the apostle Paul, using Philemon 11 as the basis for his sermon. Containing only twenty-five verses, Philemon is the shortest book in the New Testament. In it Paul considers a matter concerning Onesimus, a man who Philemon, a leader in the Colossian church in Asia Minor, had enslaved. At the time, Onesimus, whose name means "useful," "beneficial," or "profitable" in Greek, was with Paul in prison rather than with Philemon, for reasons that remain unclear. Perhaps he ran away from Philemon and subsequently encountered Paul, or Philemon could have sent Onesimus to serve Paul during his imprisonment. Either way, Paul decided to send Onesimus back to Philemon, urging Philemon to welcome Onesimus back, just as he would have welcomed Paul himself.

With more than a touch of hyperbole, Palmer praises the book of Philemon for "correctness of sentiment, for delicacy and tenderness of feeling, for a judicious and faithful regard to the rights, interests and feelings of two individuals, standing related to each other in two very distinct grades of life."[20] Portraying Philemon as a benevolent slaveholder who gave Onesimus no reason to run away, Palmer claims that "Paul gives not the slightest hint that, Philemon had, in any degree, or respect, acted unkindly to Onesimus. He [Onesimus] was bad therefore for no other reason than he would be bad."[21] Although Paul does not substantiate this charge, Palmer speculates, "It is highly probable, that he plundered his Master's property" before he ran away.[22] In contrast to his good Christian slaveholder, Onesimus, as Palmer portrays him, is ungrateful and prone to wickedness simply for the sake of wickedness. But after Onesimus escapes, Palmer imagines, he finds religion. Upon hearing the gospel, "it was the day of salvation to his hardened, guilty heart."[23] Now that Onesimus is a Christian, Palmer explains, Paul sends him back to Philemon and writes a letter on his behalf to his slaveholder.

At this point, Palmer asks the question at the heart of his sermon. "But, how shall poor Onesimus meet his master's eye, after all his ungrateful and criminal conduct? He has no excuse to make for himself, no extenuation to plead to a kind and indulgent owner."[24] In Palmer's opinion, Onesimus is completely at fault, whereas Philemon had done nothing wrong. To the white slaveholders in Charleston, who had suppressed Vesey's plot just two months before the publication of this sermon, Palmer's depiction of Philemon as an innocent and benevolent Christian slaveholder would reassure them that the plot was completely unprovoked and the result of nothing other than the inexplicable wickedness of those who had not truly found religion.

To make the case that Onesimus should submit to Philemon, Palmer quotes a New Testament passage routinely cited in proslavery literature, 1 Peter 2:18–20: "Servants, be subject to your masters with all fear; not only to the good and gentle, but also to the forward. For this is thankworthy, if a man for conscience toward God endure grief, suffering wrongfully. For what glory is it, if, when ye be buffeted for your faults, ye shall take it patiently? but if, when ye do well, and suffer for it, ye take it patiently, this is acceptable with God."[25] Palmer explains that this passage represents Paul's "injunction on Christian Servants" and that since Onesimus supposedly became a Christian after he ran away, it applied to him. Further on in his sermon, Palmer quotes Paul's directions to the enslaved in Ephesians 6:5 and Colossians 3:22–25, suggesting, condescendingly, that they reveal how "Paul and Peter have given special and plain directions to this class of people."[26]

Not coincidentally, Lionel Henry Kennedy quotes these same three biblical proof–texts in his verdicts against Vesey and his associates. As noted earlier, when sentencing Vesey, Kennedy declared, "On such texts comment is unnecessary." But Palmer's sermon suggests otherwise. Palmer offers commentary on the alleged purpose of these texts, revealing that vigorous interpretive labor is needed to ensure that readers understand these passages as justifying chattel slavery. When quoting Colossians 3:22–25, he includes a parenthetical clarification midway through verse 22 explaining what Paul means by the term "all things." Palmer quotes the verse as: "Servants, obey in all things (that is, in all things which are consistent with their duty to God, their heavenly master) your masters according to the flesh, not with eye-service, as men pleasers, but in singleness of heart, fearing God."[27] Unlike Kennedy, Palmer felt that commentary was so necessary that he inserted it directly into the quoted verse itself. A reader of the sermon would be forgiven if she or he mistook Palmer's parenthetical interpellation for Paul's own words. Palmer inserts similar parenthetical comments into a quotation from Titus 2:9–10, another proof-text popular among proslavery writers. In Palmer's sermon, this passage appears as follows: "exhort servants to be *obedient* to their own masters, and to please them well in all things; *not answering again, not purloining* (by which he means stealing,) but shewing all good fidelity; that they may adorn the doctrine of God our Saviour in all things."[28] In this case, Palmer's interpellation appears more clearly as a parenthetical statement of his own composition because it refers to the author of the quoted verses in the third person: *he* means stealing.

Palmer's commentary on texts from Colossians 3 and Titus 2 are not limited to these parenthetical insertions. Along with Colossians 3:22, he quotes verses 23–25 as, "And whatsoever ye do, do it *heartily, as to the Lord*, and not unto men, Knowing that of the Lord ye shall receive the reward of the inheritance: for ye serve the Lord Christ. But he that doeth wrong shall receive for the wrong which he hath done: and there is no respect of persons" (emphasis in the original). Palmer explains that this passage goes beyond what Paul commands in Ephesians 6:5 to introduce a "new and additional motive."[29] Focusing on the line "But he that doeth wrong shall receive for the wrong which he hath done," Palmer claims, "The servant is told, that he shall be answerable for his bad conduct as a servant, just as much as for any other bad conduct."[30] He also elaborates on the phrases that he italicized—*not answering again, not purloining*—when quoting Titus 2:9–10. Palmer alleges that talking back to their slaveholders is "a sin which they [the enslaved] are often inclined to fall into."[31] He also explains Paul's prohibition on stealing as "not pilfering, stealing, or plundering, their Masters property, or that of any other person."[32]

Aside from Philemon, Palmer saves his most detailed New Testament commentary in *Religion Profitable* for 1 Timothy 6:1–2.

These verses read: "Let as many servants as are under the yoke count their own masters worthy of all honor, that the name of God and his doctrine be not blasphemed. And they that have believing masters, let them not despise them, because they are brethren; but rather do them service, because they are faithful and beloved, partakers of the benefit." After quoting these verses, Palmer explains that servants can "count their own masters worthy of all honor" by defending their character against any slander that may be spoken when enslaved people talk about each other's slaveholders amongst themselves. Here Palmer clearly interprets these verses within the context of an antebellum society in which the slaveholder's honor is to be held in high regard.

In an aristocratic society such as the antebellum American South, one had to have equal social standing in order to offend the honor of another.[33] One might infer from this that within such a society an enslaved person can do little damage to a slaveholder's honor by badmouthing her or him. But, Palmer argues, this inference is misguided. "And if servants think, that, because they are in an inferior situation, no such great evil can grow out of their behavior, the Apostle [Paul] teaches them, that they are in a grand mistake in thinking so."[34] When an enslaved person who professes religion (meaning Christianity) slanders a slaveholder, Palmer argues, it is not innocuous gossip but rises to the level of blasphemy, as attested to by Paul in 1 Timothy 6:2: "they that have believing masters, let them not despise them, because they are brethren." Although the enslaved and slaveholder are not equal in their civil status, they are both believing Christians and thus have equal standing in this religious sense. The enslaved, as Christian sisters and brothers of their slaveholders, could injure the honor of the latter in virtue of their shared religion. By such slander, Palmer warns, the enslaved have the "power to do very great injury to the cause of religion."[35] In fact, in his opinion, such slanderous talk would qualify as blasphemy against the name of God because it involves a religious rather than social matter.

For some, this claim that the enslaved and the slaveholder are equals in Christ could raise questions about whether differences in social status should also be abolished among those who profess Christianity. But Palmer focuses on a third line from 1 Timothy 6:1–2 to preempt such ideas. He italicizes parts of the line "let the servants that have believing masters, let them not despise them, *because they are brethren*, but rather *do them service*" in order to underscore the key differences he sees between the enslaved and the slaveholder despite their shared Christianity. The enslaved must still do service for their "believing masters," notwithstanding the fact that "they and their masters belong to Christ, are saved in the same way and by the same means." The enslaved should not think that "they may become like their owners in every respect; may *dress* as well as they, and live as them in every particular."[36] In keeping with what Kennedy suggested in pronouncing his sentence on the ten enslaved persons at their trial earlier that summer, Palmer claims that a person should accept her or his station in life as assigned by divine providence "instead of despising, or attempting to be on an equality with those whom Providence has placed over them." Rather, the enslaved "are to give them greater honor, in consequence of both belonging to Christ."[37]

At first, it may seem odd that, rather than focusing on Vesey's plot, Palmer singles out the quality of a person's wardrobe to illustrate how far the enslaved have gone to claim equality with the slaveholders. Yet this remark does not appear out of nowhere. For almost a century, going back to the South Carolinian Negro Act of 1740, the white community regulated and prescribed the sort of attire that enslaved persons were allowed to wear.[38] Palmer cited the Negro Act of 1740 explicitly in his sermon when lamenting "how entirely out of place is it, when servants in their apparel and other particulars not only equal the great body of whom God and Providence have placed in the superior station; but, as is the case in too, far too many instances, far outstrip these, and even rival those in the highest rank and order of human society."[39] (A notation at the bottom of the same page reads, "The law, regulating the manner in which servants should dress, is explicit as any one in the South Carolina code.") Although 1 Timothy 6:1–2 does not mention apparel, Palmer brings it up in order to make a strained connection between this biblical text and South Carolina's legislative restrictions on people of African descent.

In Palmer's mind, attire that does not align with one's station in life is symptomatic of a disregard for divine order. Like Lionel Kennedy, he understood social hierarchies and institutions, including the slave system, to be ordained by God. Paraphrasing Ecclesiastes 3:11, he states, "Solomon observes that every thing is 'beautiful in its season.' But when things are *out of season or out of place*, disorder ensues, and ruin treads upon its heels."[40] Under such socially chaotic circumstances, people "are never satisfied unless in their dress and equipage, and other exterior things, they can appear perfectly on a level, with those who in the arrangements of Providence, have been placed in far superior circumstances."[41] Palmer asserts that many people do not follow the lesson that Paul learned in Philippians 4:11 that "in whatsoever state I am, therewith to be content." Palmer does not interpret the word "state" in this verse as a reference to one's current circumstance but rather one's divinely ordained station in life. The elite should be content to be elite, and similarly the enslaved should be content to be enslaved. He quotes

Proverbs 29:21 ("He that delicately bringeth up his servant from a child shall have him become his son at the length") to warn slaveholders of the consequences of treating the enslaved as one's children.[42] "A child ought to know, by all the treatment of a parent toward him, that he is *a child*: and a servant ought to know, in the same way, that he is *a servant*."[43] This condescending comparison of children and enslaved women or men reflects a paternalistic attitude commonplace among proslavery intellectuals. Because they believed that the enslaved, like children, were not self-reliant, they thought slavery provided the structure and discipline that the enslaved supposedly needed to survive. While Palmer does not develop this line of thinking in any detail, his colleague the Baptist minister Richard Furman used it to portray slaveholders as benevolent biblical patriarchs in his correspondence (which is examined in the next chapter) with the governor of South Carolina a few months later.

A misinterpretation of the apostle Paul's writing regarding the enslaved, in Palmer's opinion, represents an even more egregious example of social chaos. The enslaved, Palmer warns, could misinterpret biblical texts such as Colossians 4:1, which reads, "Masters, give unto your servants that which is just and equal." Building on his earlier comments on 1 Timothy 6 that a profession of Christianity does not eliminate differences in social status, Palmer argues that "just and equal" in this verse does not mean the enslaved and the slaveholder should be treated equally but that one should receive just and equal treatment as it applies to one's social status. Although he advocates for the benevolent treatment of enslaved persons, he insists that enslaved persons should receive treatment appropriate to their position as enslaved. In the aftermath of Vesey's trial, he cautions that that the Bible must be read properly lest the enslaved misinterpret it as Vesey and his associates did and advocate for equality with the white slaveholders in Charleston.

―――――

While his sermon offers detailed commentary on Philemon and the other writings from the apostle Paul that he understood as instructive for the behavior of enslaved persons, Palmer claims that "the deep root and the fertile source" of the current state of affairs in Charleston was the result of vices within the white community. Palmer characterizes these vices not only as social and moral ills but also as drains on the local economy.

The published version of Palmer's sermon concludes with a detailed appendix made up of "extracts from the report of a City Missionary in 1821," which estimated that two-thirds of the occupants of the local Poor House and the Marine Hospital "were brought there because of intemperance."[44] The takeaway for Palmer is that the sale of and taxation on alcohol in Charleston does not cover the cost of the social services required to address the consequences of alcohol consumption. In the body of the sermon, Palmer presents these statistics in the language of the prophet Isaiah, who declares that the nations are "as a drop of the bucket" in comparison to the spirit of the LORD (Isaiah 40:15). Palmer warns: "The pitiful revenue that tickles into the treasury from pecuniary exactions on these licensed manufactories of sin and misery, is but 'as a drop of the bucket,' compared with the streams that must flow out again to support the poor houses, hospitals and orphan houses peopled in three instances out of four by paupers, themselves the victims, or the offspring of those who became the victims of intemperance."[45] Palmer stresses the gravity of the situation by citing facts and figures couched in prophetic rhetoric from the Bible. To address the threats posed by moral vices he proposes the establishment of "Sabbath schools in every city, town, village, neighbourhood and settlement in the states" and the sending of "competent and well selected men of christian character into every spot and region of spiritual darkness."[46] He argues that these schools and missionary work would cost considerably less than "what is required to maintain the institutions we have spoken of."[47]

In focusing on lax moral habits such as alcohol consumption, Palmer's *Religion Profitable* effectively distances the conditions that inspired Vesey's plot from the practice of slavery, locating the root cause of Vesey's insurrection in vices within the white community rather than in the slave system itself—which Palmer considers to be a part of a divinely ordered social hierarchy. He maintains that the white community can prevent future insurrections without modifying or abolishing the practice of slavery, assuring his community that they are still in control. Palmer assumes that, in the end, white Charlestonians have the power and agency to decide the fate of the city if they only address perceived vices like drinking.

Published weeks before Kennedy and Parker's *Official Report*, Palmer's sermon represents the first full-throated theological defense of slavery in the wake of the revelation of Vesey's plot within the white community in Charleston. Through a thick network of biblical allusions and quotations, Palmer fits biblical texts to the mores and sensibilities of antebellum Charleston. The influence of his biblical interpretations would extend beyond the publication of *Religion Profitable*. Palmer's exegetical fingerprints would show up on a letter—discussed in the next chapter—that the Charleston Bible Society's board of managers sent to Governor Bennett days after the publication of Palmer's sermon.

CHAPTER FIVE

They Shall Be Your Bondmen Forever

Both thy bondmen, and thy bondmaids, which thou shalt have,
shall be of the heathen that are round about you; of them shall
ye buy bondmen and bondmaids. Moreover of the children of
the strangers that do sojourn among you, of them shall ye buy,
and of their families that are with you, which they begat in your
land: and they shall be your possession. And ye shall take
them as an inheritance for your children after you, to inherit
them for a possession; they shall be your bondmen forever.

—LEVITICUS 25:44–46

It was Sunday, July 7, 1822, five days after Denmark Vesey was
executed, and the Reverend Richard Furman, the elderly minister of First Baptist Church, stepped into his pulpit. The previous week he and his fellow clergymen Benjamin Palmer and
Artemas Boies had visited Vesey in jail. No transcripts of Furman's sermons on that Sunday survive, but a little over two
weeks later, in a letter dated July 25, Mary Lamboll Beach informed her sister Elizabeth Gilchrist that "Old doctor Furman

preached a very solemn [sermon] about a fortnight ago in the evening from those words Isa. Chap. 22.14 in Verse 'It was revealed in my ears by the Lord of Hosts surely this iniquity shall not be purged till ye be [sic] die.'"[1] At first, Beach feared that Furman's sermon on these terrifying words from Isaiah 22:14 was a prophetic judgment spelling doom for Charleston. But she was quickly assured that Furman also explained "*how the destruction of a community was to be averted or prevented*" and that he called for "a day of Public Humiliation," meaning a day on which the community humbly turned to God.[2] A few months later, Furman, in his capacity as senior vice president of the Charleston Bible Society's board of managers, helped to draft a private letter to the then governor of South Carolina, Thomas Bennett, requesting that the governor declare a "day of public humiliation and thanksgiving" in recognition of God's deliverance of the city from Vesey's plot. The request was denied.

Furman was not deterred. On Christmas Eve, 1822, he made a similar request in a second, much longer and more detailed letter—this time in his capacity as the president of the Baptist State Convention—to John L. Wilson, Bennett's successor as governor. Governor Wilson was so impressed that he endorsed the letter's publication the following spring, predicting that Furman's work will "tend to make our servants not only more contented with their lot, but more useful to their owners. The great piety and learning of DOCTOR FURMAN, his long established character with the religious of every denomination throughout our State, will at once command the respectful attention of every reader."[3] The nineteen-page letter was published as a pamphlet titled *Rev. Dr. Richard Furman's Exposition of the Views of the Baptists Relative to the Coloured Population of the United States, in a Communication to the Governor of South-*

Carolina. Over the next several decades, Furman's pamphlet would shape paternalistic ideas about slavery in the antebellum imagination.

———

In addition to its request for a day of public humiliation and thanksgiving, the earlier letter, from September 1822, to Governor Wilson's predecessor had a second objective. Acknowledging the fear in the white community that enslaved people who had read the Bible would find inspiration in its pages for future insurrections, the letter observed that this fear led some in the community to seek legislation "to prevent their learning to read [the Bible], or to use it freely."[4] The letter sought to address this fear and argue against such legislation. "The Scriptures," argued the letter's authors, "are given to Man (without respect of Persons) to make him wise unto Salvation."[5]

Furman and the other coauthors took the phrase "wise unto Salvation" from 2 Timothy 3:15: "And that from a child thou hast known the holy scriptures, which are able to make thee wise unto salvation through faith which is in Christ Jesus." Exposure to the Bible, in other words, is essential if one is to embrace Christianity. Furman and the Charleston Bible Society's board of managers believed that all people, regardless of their race or station in life, should have the opportunity to become Christians. As noted in the previous chapter, Benjamin Morgan Palmer, one of the vice presidents of the Charleston Bible Society, preached a sermon the day before the letter was written, arguing that Christianity benefited everyone. Thus, it is not surprising that the letter would declare, "all are required, by Divine Authority to read them [the scriptures]; because they contain the Words of Eternal Life. To prohibit the use of them therefore, in respect of any man or class of men, is to contradict & oppose the Divine Authority."[6]

Despite its use of biblical phrases like "wise unto salvation," the September 1822 letter explicitly quotes only one biblical text, and only in a footnote. While acknowledging that many people believe "that the Doctrines of Holy writ are unfavourable to the holding of Slaves," the authors assert that slavery's "lawfulness is positively stated in the Old Testament, & is clearly recognized in the New. In the latter a luminous Exhibition is given of Slaves."[7] Yet the letter's authors do not identify the specific texts from the Old Testament that they have in mind. The sole New Testament text, consigned to a footnote, is 1 Timothy 6:1–2. (As noted in the previous chapter, this text figured prominently in Benjamin Palmer's *Religion Profitable*. As Palmer was also a vice president of the society's board of managers, it is very likely that this citation reflects his influence. Although the letter is signed collectively as "Your Obedient Humble Servants" and the biblical references suggest Palmer's input, its main architect was Richard Furman.)[8] In the very next sentence after they footnote 1 Timothy 6:1–2, the authors argue that although slaveholders and the enslaved enjoyed "Membership together in the Christian Church," slaveholders are not obligated "to emancipate their Slaves, but to give them the things which are just, and equal, forbearing Threatening, & remembering that they also have a Master in Heaven."[9] While not a direct quote, the similarity of these lines to Colossians 4:1 is hard to miss: "Masters, give unto your servants that which is just and equal; knowing that ye also have a Master in heaven."[10]

Nevertheless, the point of the letter was not to provide a comprehensive response to those who claimed that slavery went against the teachings of the Bible. Rather, the authors invoke several of the usual biblical texts cited in support of slavery to remind Governor Bennett that, in their opinion, those who oppose slavery misuse the Bible. They write, "The Bible, Sir, as well as all other Things, good and Sacred, which have come into the hands of men, may be, & has been abused."[11] Of course, the authors assume that it is other people's biblical interpretations and not their own proslavery interpretations, that constitute an abuse of the Bible. Still, the authors' broader point is that what they consider to be an abuse of biblical texts by antislavery advocates is not a sufficient reason to restrict access to the Bible among people of African descent. "But to argue against its use, from the abuse it has suffered, is to adopt a Mode of Reasoning which is not logical, just, nor pious."[12]

It is notable that the addressee of this letter, Governor Bennett, himself enslaved three of the men—Batteau, Ned, and Rolla—who were hanged along with Vesey on July 2. Given the fact that enslaved men in his own household were intimately involved in Vesey's plot, Bennett had good reason to dismiss the seriousness of a plan that developed right under his nose. Moreover, the idea that it took an act of divine intervention to save the white citizens of Charleston would undermine James Hamilton's earlier assertion in his *Account* that "there is nothing they [Vesey and his associates] are bad enough to do, that we are not powerful enough to punish."[13] Like Bennett, Hamilton also seemed opposed to the day of public humiliation, leading Mary Lamboll Beach, as noted earlier, to assert in her July 25 letter to her sister that Hamilton "knows not God."[14] Bennett wrote a reply, dated October 1, 1822, to the letter from members of the society's board of managers. In it, he reasoned "it is a mistaken policy, which should inform them [people of African descent], that the slightest apprehension of their power is entertained, or that we believe that any effort they can possibly make, would be attended with even partial success. I do not myself believe it, and I am convinced that nine tenths of the State do not believe it."[15]

———

It was close to midnight on September 27, 1822, four days after the society's board of managers sent their letter to Governor Bennett, when a hurricane hit Charleston. Although it was not an unusually powerful storm, the death total was high. The October 7 edition of the *Charleston Mercury* estimated that in total about three hundred people died, the majority being persons of African descent.[16] The hurricane merited a mention eighteen years later, when William Gilmore Simms, a Charleston native and amateur historian, published a lengthy history of South Carolina. In a timeline of historical events, immediately after his entry on Vesey, Simms writes, "The low country visited by a destructive hurricane. Many lives and much property destroyed."[17]

To some local clergy, that Charleston survived this memorable natural disaster seemed to be yet another illustration of divine intervention. For example, on Thursday, November 7, 1822, the Reverend Arthur Buist, a member of the society's board of managers, preached a sermon titled "On the Doctrine of Particular Providence" at the First Presbyterian Church.[18] Using Psalm 97:1 as his text ("The Lord reigneth, let the earth rejoice"), he celebrated God's active and continued involvement in the world. As evidence, he emphasized the deliverance from the storm and a season of unusually good health that Charleston had recently enjoyed. But before these two examples, Buist claimed, "The first display of the Particular Providence of God which we are required this day to recognise, is that which led to the detection of a privy conspiracy."[19] He continued, "To the interposition of God we are to look for the disclosure of this atrocious combination" because God "made us acquainted with our situation, and suppressed this savage enterprise by our own instrumentality. Yes! The Lord of Hosts was with us; the God of Jacob was our defence."[20] Buist called for thanksgiving to God for "preventing a scheme which must have ended in their own extermination."[21] The following month, Furman would also connect the hurricane with Vesey's plot. When he sent the letter to Governor Wilson on Christmas Eve 1822 that became the pamphlet *Exposition of the Views of the Baptists*, he expanded the rationale for the day of public humiliation and thanksgiving as an expression of gratitude to God. It was not only for the "protection afforded them [residents of Charleston] from the horrors of an intended Insurrection," but also "the affliction they have suffered from the ravages of a dreadful Hurricane."[22]

In *Exposition of the Views of the Baptists*, Furman acknowledges antislavery interpretations of specific biblical texts only once, and it is not a text that Vesey was said to have used. Furman reports, "The Christian golden rule, of doing to others, as we would they should do to us, has been urged as an unanswerable argument against holding slaves."[23] What Furman calls the "Christian golden rule" comes from Luke 6:31: "And as ye would that men should do to you, do ye also to them likewise" (compare Matthew 7:12). "But surely this rule, is never to be urged against that order of things, which the Divine government has established." Furman objects, "A father may very naturally desire, that his son should be obedient to his orders: Is he, therefore, to obey the orders of his son?"[24] Like Lionel Kennedy, Benjamin Palmer, and his other proslavery South Carolinian contemporaries, Furman assumes that slavery, like parenthood, is part of a divinely ordained order for human societies. The comparison of a slaveholder's treatment of an enslaved person to a parent's treatment of a child reflects Furman's paternalistic understanding of slavery, which is an essential component of his pamphlet's argument.

Although Furman makes explicit reference to at least some of the biblical texts that he believes support slavery, he does not specify the texts he has in mind when he claims that "the sentiments in opposition to the holding of slaves have been attributed, by their advocates, to the Holy Scripture, and to the genius of Christianity."[25] He warns Governor Wilson that these sentiments "produce insubordination and rebellion among the slaves," but he does not clarify whether he is referring to the biblical texts that Vesey allegedly used to justify an insurrection—such as Exodus 21:16, which demands the death penalty for kidnapping and selling a person—or to other texts used by other antislavery advocates.[26] In fact, Furman not only refrains from discussing Vesey's use of the Bible; he never even mentions Vesey by name in *Exposition of the Views of the Baptists*.

To understand why, we should return to an antebellum concept of honor, which holds that one can only do damage to the honor of another when one is recognized as that person's social equal. In *Exposition of the Views of the Baptists*, Furman only counters the ideas of those whom he views as respectable or worthy opponents. In his appeal for a day of humiliation and thanksgiving, he observes that he and his colleagues "are aware, that very respectable Citizens have been averse to the proposal under consideration" before offering his rebuttal.[27] Before making his case for why the Bible condones slavery, he observes that "certain writers on politics, morals and religion, and some of them highly respectable, have advanced positions, and inculcated sentiments, very unfriendly to the principle and practice of holding slaves."[28] When he counters the idea that slavery is a "necessary evil"—a concept I shall return to later—he acknowledges that this position is held by "men, respectable for intelligence and morals."[29] Furman and other white clergy in Charleston would certainly not have included Vesey in this respectable company. Although the court that condemned Vesey recognized that he "showed great penetration and sound judgment," its members did not view Vesey as their social equal, and his antislavery biblical interpretations were thus unworthy of a direct rebuttal.[30] Vesey may merit a mention in a private letter from the society's board of managers to Governor Bennett but not in Furman's published pamphlet intended for wide dissemination.[31]

In *Exposition of the Views of the Baptists*, Furman appeals to biblical texts that the society's board of managers did not cite in their letter to Governor Bennett in September 1822. Furman focuses on Leviticus 25 to make his argument that "the right of holding slaves is clearly established In the Holy Scriptures."[32] He observes that, while Leviticus 25:40 states that Israelite servants should not be held indefinitely but released in what the Bible refers to as the "year of Jubilee," a few verses later Leviticus 25:44–46 directs the Israelites "to purchase their bond-men and bond-maids of the Heathen nations" and, "the persons purchased were to be their 'bond-men forever;' and an 'inheritance for them and their children.'"[33] This passage—which serves as the epigraph for this chapter—would become the centerpiece of Furman's biblical justification for slavery.

By the time that Furman wrote *Exposition of the Views of the Baptists*, the relevance of Leviticus 25:44–46 to chattel slavery in America had been hotly debated for over a century. As discussed in chapter 1, the New Englander Samuel Sewall cites Exodus 21:16 in his antislavery pamphlet published in 1700. The following year, however, John Saffin, another New Englander, offered a proslavery rebuttal to Sewall. Saffin cites Leviticus 25:44–46 to justify the enslavement of Africans: "Though the Israelites were forbidden (ordinarily) to make bond men and women of their own nation, but of strangers they might."[34] In 1791, in the same sermon in which Jonathan Edwards (the younger) uses Exodus 21:16 to condemn slavery (discussed in chapter 1), he offered several responses to "the principal arguments urged in favour of [slavery]."[35] One of these "principal arguments" comes from Leviticus 25. "From the divine permission given the Israelites to buy servants of the nations round about them," Edwards explains, "it is argued, that we have a right to buy the Africans and hold them in slavery. See Lev. xxv. 44–47."[36] After quoting these verses, he questions the logic of this argument. He asks whether this text "is a permission to every nation under heaven to buy slaves of the nations round about them; to us, to buy of our Indian neighbours; to them, to buy of us; to the French, to buy of the English, and to the English to buy of the French; and so through the world." He suggests that "if then this argument be valid, every man has an entire right to engage in this trade, and to buy and sell any other man of another nation, and any other man of another nation has an entire right to buy and sell him."[37]

A few years later, this text from Leviticus would make it into a lengthy entry on "Slavery" in the 1797 edition of the *Encyclopædia Britannica*.[38] This entry quotes Leviticus 25:44–46 but explains, "Unlimited as the power thus given to the Hebrews over their bond servants of heathen extraction appears to have been, they were strictly prohibited from acquiring such property by any other means than fair purchase: 'he that stealeth a man and selleth him,' said their great lawgiver [Moses], 'shall surely be put to death.'"[39] In other words, the encyclopedia's entry on slavery uses Leviticus 25 to argue that Exodus 21:16 does not prohibit slavery as long as one acquires enslaved people from "heathen" nations at a fair price rather than through kidnapping or other illegal means. Thus, according to this view, these two texts from Exodus 21 and Leviticus 25 do not contradict each other, because they both address the question of what constitutes the legal acquisition of an enslaved person rather than the question of the legitimacy of slavery in general. (In the early nineteenth century, proslavery interpretations of the legal texts in the Bible would focus increasingly on what biblical texts say about the purchase of enslaved persons or the inheritance of enslaved persons by the children of slaveholders rather than what they say about whether slavery itself is permissible.)

It would be another ten years before the United States Congress passed the Act Prohibiting Importation of Slaves of 1807, which went into effect on January 1, 1808. With the prohibition of the importation of enslaved, and potentially kidnapped, persons, one might think that the need to offer further interpretations of biblical texts condemning "manstealing" (Exodus 21:16, Deuteronomy 24:7, 1 Timothy 1:10) would become far less urgent for proslavery intellectuals. But continued debates over what is popularly known as the "Fugitive Slave Cause" in the United States Constitution (Article IV, Section 2, Clause 3) kept debates over "manstealing" alive. This clause requires the return of persons who escape slavery across state lines.[40]

On March 6, 1818, William Smith, a United States senator from South Carolina, delivered a passionate speech in support of a bill titled "An Act to Provide for Delivering Up Persons Held to Labor or Service in Any of the States or Territories, Who Shall Escape into Any Other State or Territory," which the

House of Representatives had passed. Senators who opposed the bill worried that it allowed for requests for the return of an alleged fugitive from slavery but did not provide clear guidelines for proof that such a person was in fact a fugitive from slavery in the first place. This left the door open for what the opponents of the bill characterized as "manstealing." In his speech on the Senate floor, Smith acknowledged this concern, stating, "The honorable gentleman [Senator James Burrill of Rhode Island] has spoken of the practice of the Southern people in kidnapping their free negroes, and calls them manstealers. And the gentleman from Pennsylvania [Senator Jonathan Roberts] has called them kidnappers, men-stealers, and soul drivers."[41] In response, Smith argued that the Constitution already guarantees the slaveholder's right to pursue those who escape slavery. Moreover, Smith declared, "notwithstanding the opinion of honorable gentlemen to the contrary, there have been some very respectable opinions as to the Divine authority in favor of slavery."[42] Without acknowledging that "manstealing" is talked about in the Bible or that antislavery advocates frequently invoked biblical texts, Smith discussed Noah's curse (Genesis 9:25–27, which I examine in chapter 6) and contended that "he would show from the bible itself that slavery was permitted by divine authority, and for that purpose he would open the XXV chap, of Leviticus."[43] After quoting Leviticus 25:39–45, he continued, "This, Mr. President, is the word of God, as given to us in the holy bible, delivered by the Lord himself to his chosen servant, Moses. It might be hoped this would satisfy the scruples of all who believe in the divinity of the bible."[44]

Smith's impassioned speech was not enough to get the bill through the Senate. It did, however, impress his constituents back in South Carolina. Four years later, Edwin C. Holland, a native of Charleston and the editor of the local newspaper the *Charleston Times*, quoted Smith's discussion of Leviticus 25 in a pamphlet titled *Refutation of the Calumnies Circulated against the Southern & Western States Respecting the Institution and Existence of Slavery among Them*.[45] Copyrighted on October 29, 1822, a little less than two months before Furman's letter to Governor Wilson, and written under the pseudonym "A South Carolinian," Holland's eighty-six-page pamphlet provided a vigorous defense against criticisms of the court that tried and convicted Vesey.[46] Holland argued that Vesey's plot was part of a larger ongoing history of insurrections. He quotes from reports on various insurrections in the Carolinas dating back to 1711, but he does not provide details about Vesey's plot because "[t]he particulars of this are too fresh in the memory of all to need any repetition. It was a subject of deep and breathless anxiety, and its features are preserved with the most scrupulous accuracy in the memory of those who were to have been the victims of its diabolical brutality."[47] Likewise, he does not discuss or offer alternative interpretations of specific biblical texts used by Vesey in support of his plot because Holland claims that those "who are acquainted with the rise and progress of that nefarious plot, know how blasphemously the word of God was tortured, in order to sanction the unholy butchery that was contemplated."[48] For Holland, quoting at length Senator Smith's analysis of biblical texts was a sufficient illustration that the Bible supports slavery. Holland did not offer his own comments about the Bible.

The popularity of Leviticus 25 among proslavery intellectuals was well established by the time that Furman wrote his *Exposition of the Views of the Baptists*, so it is not surprising that he would reference this text. His particular interpretation of this text, however, would be groundbreaking for supporters of slavery.

Immediately after Furman cites Leviticus 25:44–46, he states
that enslaved persons who are not Israelites lived "in the families of the Hebrews as servants, or slaves, born in the house, or
bought with money."[49] Furman reasons that one could also be
born into slavery because, in Acts 22:28, the apostle Paul claims,
"I was free born." For Furman, the need to specify that one is
free born would not make sense unless the biblical authors assumed that one could also be born into slavery. In Furman's
opinion, the significance of Leviticus 25:44–46 was not simply
that it allowed for the purchase of enslaved people but that,
whether one is purchased or born into slavery, she or he is considered a member of the family.

Legal material in the Bible frequently includes enslaved men
and women (which the King James Version refers to as "man-
servants" and "maidservants") in lists of members of Israelite
households. For example, one of the Ten Commandments requires the entire household to observe the Sabbath. It states,
"Thou shalt not do any work, thou, nor thy son, nor thy
daughter, thy manservant, nor thy maidservant, nor thy cattle,
nor thy stranger that is within thy gates" (Exodus 20:10; cf. Deuteronomy 5:14). In Deuteronomy 12:12, God commands the
Israelites to "rejoice before the LORD your God, ye, and your
sons, and your daughters, and your menservants, and your
maidservants" (for similar lists, cf. Deuteronomy 12:18, 16:11–14,
24:17–22). Households in ancient Israel consisted of several
generations living under the authority of the senior male member, or patriarch. The patriarch was responsible for all the
household dependents, including children, spouses, enslaved
persons, and so on.

In Furman's mind, an antebellum slaveholder resembles a biblical patriarch. Furman invokes this biblical household model in response to the charge that slavery is inherently cruel. He admits, "Magistrates, husbands, and fathers, have proved tyrants" but contends, "[t]his does not prove, that magistracy, the husband's right to govern, and parental authority, are unlawful and wicked."[50] Using paternalistic language, he claims, "A bond-servant may be treated with justice and humanity as a servant; and a master may, in an important sense, be the guardian and even father of his slaves."[51] He continues, "They become a part of his family, (the whole forming under him a little community) and the care of ordering it, and of providing for its welfare, devolves on him. The children, the aged, the sick, the disabled, and the unruly, as well as those, who are capable of service and orderly, are the objects of his care."[52] As with biblical patriarchs such as Abraham, Isaac, or Jacob, the antebellum adult male slaveholder shoulders responsibility for the welfare of his dependents, including those whom he enslaves. It is, in Furman's opinion, his biblically mandated duty to support these "objects of his care."

A paternalistic approach to slavery viewed it as an extension of domestic life on the plantation. This idea assumes that the patriarch's dependents—including free women and free male and female children—willingly consented to his authority as head of the household. As the historian William W. Freehling explains, slaveholders who claimed to be patriarchs "demanded that their slaves act out a charade of consent to that claim."[53] Under this charade, slavery was understood as a mutually beneficial arrangement between the caring patriarch and his dependents. The influence of this idea on Furman is evident when, immediately after listing the family dependents for which the patriarch must provide, he writes, "The labour of [the dependents capable of service], is applied to the benefit of those [dependents unable to serve: children, the aged, the sick, the disabled, and the unruly], and to their own support, as well as to that of the master."[54] For his part, the slaveholder was responsible for his dependents and all their expenses.[55]

Imagined as a benevolent patriarch, the slaveholder in this allegedly biblically based familial structure also contributes to an important civic good beyond the domestic realm. In *Religion Profitable*, Palmer had already raised concern over the high costs of taxes used for social services such as poorhouses or hospitals to care for those affected by vices that he believed plagued Charleston. As discussed in the previous chapter, Palmer proposed that government-subsidized Sabbath schools would curb these expenses by teaching morality to the public. Furman also acknowledges that there is "a great public expense, in a free community, by taxes, benevolent institutions, bettering houses, and penitentiaries" but contends that under the slave system the cost "lies here on the master, to be performed by him, whatever contingencies may happen; and often occasions much expense, care and trouble, from which the servants are free."[56] In other words, Furman shifts the financial burden from the public to the domestic sphere through the supposed benevolence of the slaveholding patriarch.

Furman's paternalistic approach illustrates the change in strategy that Egerton and Paquette describe when they write, "Charleston's theologians took a leading role in moving the defense of slavery in the South away from the soft ground of necessary evil or temporary expedient to a much firmer, more sophisticated biblical and historical defense of the institution as a positive good."[57] The theory of slavery as a "necessary evil" held that slavery was a curse that slaveholders did not create but that they inherited nonetheless. Although they were not responsible for slavery's existence, slaveholders had to ameliorate its effects through the compassionate treatment of the enslaved.[58] Holland reflects this idea in his *Refutation of the Calumnies* when he writes, "It must be conceded by every fair and candid reasoner, who is at all acquainted with the history of our country, that the introduction of this mischievous and unhappy institution [slavery] is not imputable to the present generation, nor are we answerable either to heaven, or to earth, for its existence."[59] Furman acknowledges this idea when he writes that some believe "that holding slaves is indeed indefensible, but that to us it is necessary; and must be supported."[60] Nevertheless, he rejects this idea in favor of a conception of slavery as not an evil to be ameliorated but a domestic and civic good for which he finds a biblical precedent in texts that list the enslaved among members of the household.

———

For those who held to a paternalistic understanding of slavery, Vesey's plot represented a direct challenge to the pretense that enslaved people consented to this system. When collectively sentencing the ten enslaved defendants to death, Lionel Kennedy expressed shock that they did not acknowledge how well they had things. He reminds them that "in no age or country has the condition of slaves been milder or more humane than your own. You are, with few exceptions, treated with kindness, and enjoy every comfort compatible with your situation. You are exempt from many of the miseries, to which *the poor* are subject throughout the world."[61] Kennedy claims that they were "[r]eared by the hand of kindness, and fostered by a master who assumed many of the duties of a parent."[62] Following the paternalistic myth that slavery provided structure for the enslaved because, like children, they were incapable of governing themselves, he admonishes the defendants. "Such men as you, are in general, as ignorant as you are vicious, without any settled principles, and possessing but few of the virtues of civilized life; you would soon, therefore, have degenerated into a horde of barbarians, incapable of any government."[63] Yet, despite Kennedy's protests, the sheer number of enslaved persons that were involved in Vesey's plot ran counter to slaveholders' insistence that those whom they enslaved willingly consented to this arrangement.

It should be no surprise, then, that, after Vesey's plot was exposed, many supporters of slavery felt that paternalism resulted in excessive leniency toward enslaved persons. In late 1822, Nicholas Herbemont, a French immigrant to Charleston, wrote a pamphlet titled *Observations Suggested by the Late Occurrences in Charleston*, published under the pseudonym "A Member of the Board of Public Works." He asserts, "[I]t is a well known fact that all blacks concerned in the late attempt at an insurrection belonged to very indulgent masters," and concludes that "[f]rom these undisputable facts it would appear that great severity is the surest means of keeping slaves in due subjection."[64] James Hamilton tried to counter charges that slavery in Charleston was too mild when, as noted earlier, he states in the preface of his *Account* that his pamphlet would show "that there is nothing they are bad enough to do, that we are not powerful enough to punish."[65] In publishing the trial transcripts, Hamilton wanted to demonstrate to the public that the court, and by extension Charleston's slaveholding community, was firmly in control of those that they enslaved. Far from indulging the enslaved, they were fully capable of dispensing severe punishment when the need arose.

Written in the center of this firestorm, Furman's *Exposition of the Views of the Baptists* sought not just to provide a biblical defense of slavery itself but also of paternalistic approaches to slavery. Near the end of his pamphlet, Furman connects paternalism to the objectives of the earlier letter from the Charleston Bible Society's board of managers when he writes that slaveholders "being the heads of families, are bound, on principles of moral and religious duty, to give these servants religious instruction; or at least, to afford them opportunities, under proper regulations to obtain it."[66] His pamphlet supports the letter's argument against draconian restrictions on religious instruction for those of African descent. Imagined as a biblical patriarch, the slaveholder bears responsibility for ensuring that members of his household, including those members whom he enslaves, have access to religious instruction.

Palmer's *Religion Profitable* rehearses many of the standard arguments used in biblically informed defenses of slavery and invokes a far greater number of biblical texts than Furman's pamphlet does. By contrast, Furman's partial quotations from Leviticus 25:44–46 and Acts 22:28 are the only biblical texts in *Exposition of the Views of the Baptists* that Palmer had not already discussed in *Religion Profitable*. Yet, this is because Furman's larger goal is to show the biblical foundations of paternalism rather than slavery in general.

CHAPTER SIX

For He Is His Money

And if a man smite his servant, or his maid, with a rod,
and he die under his hand; he shall be surely punished.
Notwithstanding, if he continue a day or two, he shall
not be punished: for he is his money.

—EXODUS 21:20–21

In July 1823, a year after Vesey's death, prominent white citizens
of Charleston who were concerned that laws intended to control people of African descent were not rigorously enforced created an organization called the South Carolina Association. An
article in the July 24, 1823, edition of the *Charleston Courier*
claims that the South Carolina Association aimed "to aid the
execution of the laws founded upon the local and peculiar policy of South Carolina."[1] The organization's members included
many of those associated with Vesey's trial, such as Benjamin
Elliott, Lionel Henry Kennedy, and even George Warren Cross,
Vesey's attorney at his trial.[2] One of the South Carolina Association's first initiatives was to buttress a law, popularly known as
the Negro Seaman Act, passed by the South Carolina legislature
shortly after Vesey's plot was uncovered. The law "allowed local

authorities to imprison free black sailors or ship employees arriving in South Carolina ports until their ships were ready to depart,"[3] thereby—at least in theory—preventing sailors from spreading antislavery propaganda among people of African descent in Charleston. When enforcement of the Negro Seaman Act lapsed, the South Carolina Association moved to strengthen law enforcement and provide attorneys to defend against challenges to the law.[4] The South Carolina Association had a rapid impact within the white community of Charleston. The title page of *Practical Considerations Founded on the Scriptures, Relative to the Slave Population of South-Carolina*, an 1823 proslavery pamphlet written by an Episcopalian minister at Charleston's Saint Michael's Church named Frederick Dalcho, under the pseudonym "a South Carolinian," indicates that the author dedicated the pamphlet to the South Carolina Association. The pamphlet both acknowledges the widespread influence of and support for the South Carolina Association and takes issue with the view among the association's most vociferous supporters that draconian restrictions must be placed on the religious education of those of African descent. The pamphlet makes a case that while the Bible does not prohibit slavery, it requires religious instruction for everyone, including enslaved persons. In the opening pages of the pamphlet, Dalcho declares:

I profess myself to be a decided advocate for the religious instruction of our slaves. Jesus Christ commanded his Apostles, to "preach the Gospel *to every creature*."—*Mark*, xvi, 15. And again, "That repentance and remission of sins should be preached in his name, *among all nations*, beginning at Jerusalem.—*Luke* xxiv, 47. Can I, then, withhold my prayer to heaven, that the whole human race, without distinction of colour, or nation, may be brought to a knowledge of God their Redeemer, and be saved? I know from the Scriptures, that "God would have *all men* to be saved, and come to the knowledge of the truth, as it is in Jesus."—1 *Tim*. ii. 4.—*Eph*. iv. 21. God, then, requires it.[5]

This passage provides a good example of Dalcho's style of argument throughout the pamphlet. He makes a theological claim and follows it with several supporting biblical quotations, along with their chapter and verse references. Richard Furman makes the same argument for the religious education of enslaved people in his pamphlet *Exposition of the Views of the Baptists*.[6] But, unlike Dalcho, Furman directly cites only three biblical texts in his entire pamphlet (Leviticus 25:44–46, Acts 22:28, and 2 Timothy 6:1–2), although he occasionally uses phrases that come from the Bible such as "wise unto salvation" (2 Timothy 3:15) and paraphrases texts such as Colossians 4:1. Dalcho, by contrast, cites 2 Timothy 3:15 in its entirety to support his position: "Can, then, a knowledge of the religion of the Bible, be useless to any person, or particularly improper for our servants? St. Paul asserts, that 'the Holy Scriptures, which are able to make thee wise unto salvation through faith which is in Christ Jesus. All scripture is given by inspiration of God, and is profitable for doctrine, for reproof, for correction, for instruction in righteousness.' 2 *Tim. iii.* 15. 16."[7]

Dalcho points out the paucity of biblical references in Furman's pamphlet. He argues that this scantiness places Furman's justification for slavery and his argument for the religious instruction of enslaved persons "on insufficient ground."[8] His own pamphlet, which he peppers with more biblical quotations and allusions than can be considered here, is intended as a rectification.

Early in his pamphlet, Dalcho alleges that South Carolina has been infiltrated by "persons born and educated in all the prejudices of non-slave-holding countries, and mere itinerants here for a few winter months."[9] He then claims, "It is known to many, that field Negroes have been collected and addressed, without the knowledge or consent of their masters."[10] Dalcho does not identify these alleged itinerants by name, but he may have had Lorenzo Dow in mind. Dow, a white antislavery Methodist preacher convicted of libel by a Charleston court in 1821, was said to have preached to enslaved people in the fields.[11] Vesey and his associates knew of Dow. In a confession after the plot was uncovered, Bacchus Hammet refers to Dow by name while recounting a conversation with Vesey during a meeting at Vesey's home. "Denmark asked me who I belonged to and my name, Perault immediately answered 'Bacchus belonging to Mr. Hammet,' Denmark asked me which Hammet, I said Mr. Benjamin Hammet, the gentleman who put old Lorenzo Dow in jail."[12] In Dalcho's opinion, itinerants such as Dow are well meaning but ignorant of the laws and customs of South Carolina. "These persons come here, we must believe, with the best intentions, and full of missionary zeal; but they come full-fraught with speculative notions of personal liberty, and would change 'times and laws' to promote, what *they* conceive to be a correct, and religious, view of the subject."[13] The phrase "change 'times and laws'" comes from the first half of Daniel 7:25, an apocalyptic text featuring a vision of a powerful ruler who speaks against God: "And he shall speak great words against the most High, and shall wear out the saints of the most High, and think to change times and laws." For Dalcho, antislavery advocates from out of state are comparable to blasphemers who challenge God and would seek to change divinely decreed laws. Like Lionel Kennedy, Benjamin Palmer, and many others, Dalcho understood the slavery system in Charleston as a divinely ordained social hierarchy. Antislavery itinerants seeking to change the legal and social structure that God endorsed according to "what *they* conceive to be a correct, and religious, view" joined the company of the cosmic forces warring against God's saints.

Dalcho also claims that plantation owners would be willing to release the people they enslaved if it were feasible economically to do so. Unlike Furman, Dalcho deems slavery to be a "necessary evil" that current slaveholders did not institute but simply inherited.[14] "We deprecate the evil which attends it. It has descended to us; we have not produced it," Dalcho laments. "We would most willingly apply the remedy, if we knew what it was."[15] He considers various ideas for the manumission of the enslaved but admits that they are not viable economically. For example, he imagines that slaveholders would agree to have non-slaveholding states purchase southern plantations and the enslaved people who worked on them and, then, "send the latter to Africa under the patronage of the Colonization Society, a scheme that would require free states to provide massive monetary compensation for slaveholding States and huge expenditures for repatriation of all former slaves."[16]

Dalcho turned to Exodus 21, the same chapter that Vesey allegedly used to justify his plot, to provide a biblical justification for his notion that emancipation would need to be accompanied by the financial compensation of slaveholders. He zeroes in on Exodus 21:20–21, the text that serves as this chapter's epigraph. Although, in context, these verses regulate how a slaveholder may treat an enslaved person, Dalcho invokes them to declare, "As to parting with them [the enslaved] without an equivalent, is out of the question: for our servants are our money: Exod. xxi. 20. 21. and we shall never choose beggary for ourselves and our families, when it is left to our choice. Our lands might as well be asked of us as our Negroes, because they once belonged to the Indians."[17] Dalcho focuses only on the final line of Exodus 21:21 ("for he is his money"), which he paraphrases as "for our servants are our money." Dalcho's paraphrase shifts the context of Exodus 21:20–21 from regulations on the behavior of a slaveholder who strikes an enslaved person to a biblical endorsement of slavery as the foundation for South Carolina's economy. He also extends the logic of the "necessary evil" theory of slavery to land rites by recognizing that the land that he and his contemporaries now possess "once belonged to the Indians." Although they may not have taken the land themselves, Dalcho maintains that they would voluntarily reduce themselves to a state of extreme poverty if they gave the land up.[18]

———

Dalcho was well aware that antislavery advocates were unconvinced by these types of economic arguments because, in his words, they insist "we have no right to hold these people in slavery, because, by nature, they are as free as ourselves." But he retorts, "What they were intended to be by nature, we can know nothing, but from what the Bible has revealed."[19] Here, Dalcho turns to the Bible in search of an origins story for slavery and provides a detailed analysis of the story of Noah's curse of his grandson Canaan in the book of Genesis. The curse occurs at the end of Genesis 9, shortly after Noah, his family, and the animals depart the ark after the floodwaters have receded. Dalcho begins his analysis by quoting the King James rendition of Genesis 9:20–28:

And Noah began to be an husbandman, and he planted a vineyard: And he drank of the wine, and was drunken; and he was uncovered within his tent. And Ham, the father of Canaan, saw the nakedness of his father, and told his two brethren without. And Shem and Japheth took a garment, and laid it upon both their shoulders, and went backward, and covered the nakedness of their father; and their faces were backward, and they saw not their father's nakedness. And Noah awoke from his wine, and knew what his younger son had done unto him. And he said, Cursed be Canaan; a servant of servants shall he be unto his brethren. And he said, Blessed be the LORD God of Shem; and Canaan shall be his servant. God shall enlarge Japheth, and he shall dwell in the tents of Shem; and Canaan shall be his servant. And Noah lived after the flood three hundred and fifty years.

Dalcho calls attention to the fact that, although Noah miraculously knew what Ham did when he woke up, he nevertheless curses Ham's son named Canaan rather than Ham himself. Dalcho understands Noah's words as a hereditary curse upon Ham's descendants, comparing this curse to other biblical prophecies directed at an individual but affecting his descendants. "The prophecy of Noah, like that of the Angel concerning Ishmael [Genesis 16:11–12, 17:20], and those concerning Esau [Genesis 27:39–40], and the twelve Patriarchs [Genesis 49]," Dalcho observes, "was to be fulfilled, not in the individuals named, but nationally in their descendants."[20]

Noah's curse, Dalcho reasons, is still in effect and continues to this day because, unlike other curses in the Bible, "we find no prophecy which removes the curse of servitude from the descendants of Ham and Canaan."[21] As examples of other prophecies that removed previous curses, he cites passages from Amos, Micah, Zechariah, and Luke that predict the return of previously exiled people to Israel. Dalcho concedes, however, that the descendants of Ham and Canaan are cursed with servitude only in this life and not in the afterlife. "The curse did not extend to the soul and eternity, but merely to their bodies and the present life. No individual, therefore, was deprived of the possibility of salvation."[22] This is why Dalcho believed that enslaved people should have access to Christian education. It could help to secure their salvation in the life to come.

Dalcho offers a lengthy explanation for why we should identify the descendants of Ham and Canaan as people of African descent. Just after Noah's curse, Genesis 10 records the genealogies of his three sons, Shem, Ham, and Japheth. The genealogy for Ham lists four sons, including Canaan and his three previously unmentioned older brothers: "And the sons of Ham; Cush, and Mizraim, and Phut, and Canaan" (Genesis 10:6). All of the sons except Canaan are associated with territory in northern Africa: Cush with Ethiopia, Mizraim with Egypt, and Phut with Libya. For Dalcho, this implies that, after the flood, Ham's descendants repopulated Africa, with the descendants of Noah's other sons, Shem and Japheth, repopulating territory outside of Africa.

Dalcho then makes a complicated and strained argument to show that the descendants of Ham's youngest son, Canaan, ended up in Africa along with those of Ham's three other sons.[23] He begins by recalling God's promise of the land of Canaan to Abram and his offspring. Abram, later called Abraham, is a descendant of Noah's son Shem, according to a genealogy in Genesis 11:10–27. A few chapters later, God appears to Abram and declares, "Unto thy seed have I given this land, from the river of Egypt unto the great river, the river Euphrates . . . [the land of] the Amorites, and the *Canaanites*, and the Girgashites, and the Jebusites" (Genesis 15:18, 21; emphasis added). Since God granted the land of Canaan to Abram, a descendant of Shem,

Dalcho reasons that the descendants of Ham, including the Canaanites, the Amorites, the Girgashites, and the Jebusites, had
no legitimate, divinely sanctioned claim to the same land. For
Dalcho, they were in fact usurpers, and justly expelled from the
land of Canaan by Shem's descendants, the Israelites, under the
leadership of Moses's successor Joshua after their long enslavement in Egypt.[24]

In Dalcho's mind, then, the Canaanites who were conquered
by the Israelites in the book of Joshua were the descendants of
Ham. "[T]he sons of Canaan usurped Palestine, as well as the
sons of Cush, under Nimrod, the land of Shinaar, or Babel; both
being allotted to Shemites by divine decree. And this furnishes
an additional proof of the justice of the expulsion of the Canaanites by the Israelites, the rightful possessors of the land of
Palestine, under Moses, Joshua, and their successors; when the
original grant was renewed to Abraham.—*Gen.* xv. 13 *to end.*"[25]
In other words, the Israelites, as descendants of Shem, through
Abraham, were simply taking back the land that the God prom-
ised to their ancestor from the descendants of Ham and Canaan
when they battled the Canaanites in the book of Joshua.

Furthermore, Dalcho asserts, some of the Canaanites who
survived Joshua's conquest fled to Africa. Dalcho turned to
sources from late antiquity for validation. Citing Procopius, a
Byzantine historian who lived in the sixth century CE, Dalcho
claims, "[M]any of the Girgashites, Jebusites, and other Canaa-
nitish nations, settled at Tingis, now Tangier, in Africa. 'There,'
[Procopius] says, 'nigh a large fountain, appears two pillars of
white stone, having this inscription engraved on them in Phoenician characters: *We are those who fled from the face of Joshua,
the son of Nun, the robber.'*"[26] Although Dalcho acknowledges
issues with the historical reliability of this inscription, he bol-
sters his argument by citing several earlier Christian writers

who, he believes, make similar claims. For example, he writes, "Augustine, Bishop of Hippo in Africa, testifies, that 'if any of the boors in the neighbourhood of Hippo or Carthage was asked who he was, or of what country, he answered that he was a Canaanite.' Eusebius also asserts that the Canaanites, who were routed by Joshua, led colonies into Africa, and settled at Triimli."[27] Thus, concludes Dalcho, the surviving descendants of Canaan, Ham's cursed son, fled from the land of Canaan to Africa. There, they joined the descendants of Ham's other three sons (Cush, Mizraim, and Phut).

After offering this poorly constructed argument for why people of African descent come from Ham's cursed son Canaan, Dalcho emphasizes the permanence of the curse of slavery. He quotes from Leviticus 25:44-46, which, as discussed in the previous chapter, is one of the few biblical texts also quoted in Furman's *Exposition of the Views of the Baptists*. Citing the part of this text that allows for the permanent enslavement of people from other nations, Dalcho declares, "Here is God's express command to the Israelites, to hold slaves forever, provided they were not of their brethren."[28] This text, in Dalcho's opinion, further justifies the continued practice of slavery in South Carolina. He then turns to the New Testament and spends several pages quoting the standard texts from the Epistles used in many proslavery arguments (for example, Colossians 3:22–24, Ephesians 6:5–9, the book of Philemon, Titus 2:9–10, 1 Peter 2:18).[29] Like Palmer, he finds support in these texts for his argument that embracing Christianity does not change one's status as enslaved or free in this life.

After quoting all the biblical texts that he feels support slavery, he concludes, "There is nothing; in the law of God, which can, in the slightest manner, justify the disobedience and revolt of slaves."[30] This is a clear reference to Vesey's plot. Although he never refers to Vesey by name anywhere in his pamphlet, he refers to Vesey's plot indirectly as "the unhappy event which gave rise to these remarks."[31] Dalcho follows the practice of other proslavery theologians in Charleston such as Palmer and Furman in not refuting Vesey's biblical interpretations directly. Instead, he objects to leaders in the African Church "who will expound the Scriptures according to their own views, or excite the malignant passions of their deluded hearers, by, perhaps, an unintentional, if not a designed, misconstruction of the sacred page."[32] Without referring to Vesey's use of the Bible directly, this pamphlet offers a riposte to Vesey's association of Joshua and the Israelites with people of African descent in Charleston and the Canaanites with the white residents of Charleston. In contrast, Dalcho made dubious historical arguments about the cursed Canaanites that associated them with people of African descent rather than white slaveholders, as Vesey had done.[33]

———

When sentencing Vesey and his associates to death, Lionel Kennedy stressed the peaceful aspect of Christianity to allege that the defendants sought to mislead their followers with their interpretations of the Bible and their religious instruction. Dalcho adopted a similar line, but unlike Kennedy, he argued that enslaved persons must receive proper religious instruction— meaning instruction from proslavery clergy like himself. "Religious instruction would set them right," he asserts, "Besides, ignorance renders them subject to deception. An intelligent knave might easily excite their fears, or their passions, and lead them into mischief."[34] Dalcho may very well have had Vesey or the antislavery itinerants in mind when he refers to "an intelligent knave," but, in any case, he believes the religious needs of enslaved people are better served by what he refers to as "regular" clergy: "I do not believe that there are many well informed religious men, who seriously object to the rational instruction of Negroes, in the leading doctrines of the Gospel, by regular, and judicious Clergymen belonging to the state. The objection lies against their injudicious instruction. It will not be denied, that, in every denomination of Christians in Carolina, there are Clergymen who possess sufficient learning, piety, judgement, patriotism, discretion, and willingness of disposition, to enter seriously into this part of their duty."[35]

To support this claim, Dalcho notes that none of people convicted of involvement in Vesey's plot were members of his Episcopal Church in Charleston. "*None of the Negroes belonging to the Protestant Episcopal Church were concerned in the late conspiracy,*" he declared. "Is it because in the sober, rational, sublime and evangelical worship of the Protestant Episcopal Church, there is nothing to inflame the passions of the ignorant enthusiast; nothing left to the crude, undigested ideas of illiterate black class-leaders?"[36]

Dalcho's call for the right sort of religious instruction for people of African descent by "regular, and judicious Clergymen" and his promotion of the worship practiced in his own church follows an argument made by Furman a few months earlier. In *Exposition of the Views of the Baptists*, Furman claims that "in the late projected scheme for producing an insurrection among us, there were very few of those who were, as members attached to regular churches, (even within the sphere of its operations) who appear to have taken a part in the wicked plot, or indeed to whom it was made known; of some churches it does not appear, that there were any."[37] Dalcho cites these lines as part of a larger quotation from Furman's pamphlet in a footnote to support Dalcho's assertion that Vesey's plot "had its origin and seat, chiefly in the *African Church*, which was entirely composed of negroes, under preachers of their own colour."[38] Seven years later, in 1830, James Osgood Andrew of Trinity Methodist Church in Charleston declared that "not a solitary member of this Church, in regular standing, had the slightest concern in the business [Vesey's plot]."[39] In other words, white clergy from Episcopal, Baptist, and Methodist churches all claimed that the members of African descent in their congregations had little or nothing to do with Vesey's plot.

Dalcho explains that none of the people of African descent belonging to his church were involved in the plot because of the way worship was organized in the Protestant Episcopal Church. The class leaders of African descent in his church followed "the regular course prescribed in the Book of Common Prayer, for the day. Hymns or Psalms out of the same book were sung, and a printed sermon read. White persons were often present on these occasions. No extemporary address, exhortation, or prayer, was permitted, or used."[40] This closely proscribed format for worship, Dalcho implies, minimized any unscripted discussion about biblical or religious endorsements of a revolt against slaveholders.

As discussed in chapter 1, Vesey knew that Benjamin Palmer and other local white clergy created separate catechisms for their congregants of African descent. Building on the model of religious instruction in his own church, Dalcho made a similar suggestion. He proposed that people of African descent should receive their religious instruction not directly from the Bible, but instead from "plain and practical, and, at the same time, interesting, moral tracts."[41] These tracts would include "a course of practical lessons [that] might be *selected* from the Bible, particularly from the historical books, the Psalms and Proverbs, but principally from the New Testament, and proper prayers composed, adapted to their condition and necessities."[42] Such selective use of biblical texts would of course provide congregants of African descent with an incomplete and heavily redacted exposure to the contents of the Bible. Through exposure to a carefully arranged selection of biblical texts rather than through direct exposure to the Bible itself, these congregants could easily come away with the impression that the Bible's primary message was an endorsement of slavery and a condemnation of revolt or any attempt to change one's station in life.

Epilogue

NO RESPECTER OF PERSONS

Then Peter opened his mouth, and said, Of a truth I perceive
that God is no respecter of persons.

—ACTS 10:34

It was 1850 and Denmark Vesey had been dead for over a quar-
ter century. Yet the mass executions that took place in the immediate wake of his suppressed plot were still vivid in the minds
of those who had been living in Charleston in 1822. Nearly three
decades later, an author writing under the pseudonym "A Colored American" penned a particularly graphic account of the
executions of the twenty-two men carried out on July 26, 1822.
He wrote that "owing to some bad arrangement in preparing
the ropes—some of which were too long, others not properly
adjusted so as to choke effectually the sufferers to death, but so
as to give them the power of utterance, whilst their feet could
touch the ground—they, in their agony of strangulation, begged
earnestly to be dispatched."[1] Earlier accounts had also indicated
that some of the hangings were botched. In 1830, Peter Neilson,
a Scottish writer recollecting his time in the United States, described the hangings as conducted "in a very bungling manner,"
because "the plank upon which the wretches stood not descend-

ing low enough, several of them were kept for some minutes with their feet dangling on it."[2] In a letter to her sister dated July 27, 1822, Mary Lamboll Beach admitted that with "some of the poor Sufferers the business was managed very badly indeed" and that in at least one case "he was shot at last, said by accident, but in pity I suppose to end his suffering."[3] But the author identified as "A Colored American" claimed that the condemned men were not shot by accident or out of pity. Instead, this author's account emphasized the brutality displayed toward people of African descent by William Dove, the captain of the City Guard who had arrested Vesey on June 22, 1822. After the hangings did not kill those sentenced to die, the author claims that it "was done with pistol-shot by the Captain of the City Guard, who was always prepared for such an emergency; i.e. shooting slaves."[4]

According to this author, this was not the first time that Captain Dove fatally shot a person of African descent. The author claims to have witnessed Dove "shoot down dead a colored man, who did not give him the slightest offence." The author elaborates, "The man whom he shot was in some difficulty with his wife, and the Captain passing by at the time, ordered him to surrender; but the man declining to obey his order, was shot, and fell into the arms of death for his temerity."[5] Writing twenty-two years after William Dove's death in 1828, the author decried the fact that Dove was never held accountable for this murder. Alluding to Acts 10:34, in which the apostle Peter declares that God does not show preference for one group of people over another, the author warned that slaveholding states are very lucky that the enslaved do not have the same resources as those who declared independence from England in 1776. Acts 10:34, which in the King James Version uses "respect" as an old-fashioned expression for preference or partiality, became a standard citation in antislavery literature. It was used to dispute the notion, reflected in the proslavery literature discussed throughout this book, that God's created order favored the slaveholders over the enslaved.[6] "Oh! when we reflect that God is no respecter of persons," the author exclaimed, "we are forcibly brought to this conclusion, that it is surpassing fortunate for these States that the slaves generally have not the endowment of those eminent men, whose patriotism led on the sons of 1776 to deeds of renown."[7] For this author, it was simply the slaveholder's good fortune, and not God's providence, that saved them from Vesey's plot, despite what the Kennedys, Palmers, Furmans, or Dalchos of the world would have their readers believe.

————

Charleston's Hampton Park, named for Wade Hampton, a Confederate general who was later elected governor of South Carolina, is currently the location of a controversial statue of Denmark Vesey. The statue was installed in 2014 after a passionate campaign for it that lasted nearly two decades during which the construction of the monument faced fierce opposition. Created by an African American sculptor named Ed Dwight, the statue imagines what Vesey might have looked like, a man proudly standing with his head held high. He holds his hat and a carpenter's bag in his right hand while clutching a Bible to his side with his left hand.[8]

Just over a year after the statue's installation, on April 19, 2015, a commemoration was held in Hampton Park to celebrate the 150th anniversary of the end of the Civil War. The Reverend and South Carolina State Senator Clementa C. Pinckney, pastor of Emanuel African Methodist Episcopal Church, was among the speakers on that brisk April day. In his remarks, Pinckney called

FIGURE 7. Denmark Vesey monument in Hampton Park, Charleston.

attention to his church's historical connection with Vesey and the events of 1822: "It was in 1822 that Mother Emanuel was standing strong and one of its members and ministers Denmark Vesey had this wonderful, crazy idea that the Constitution actually was correct that freedom was for all people. Little did he know that there would be such a backlash when he wanted to make sure that freedom was for all people, and those of you may know that after the Denmark Vesey incident, Demark Vesey and others were rounded up, they were imprisoned and later killed."[9] Pinckney envisioned Vesey as a patriot, deeply invested in achieving the ideals stated in the United States Constitution and willing to fight "to make sure that freedom was for all people." On this point, he agreed with the author identified as "A Colored American" who referred to those who were executed for their alleged participation in Vesey's plot as "worthy patriots."[10]

Yet, the pseudonymous "A Colored American" and Pinckney differed on the implications for Charleston of the apostle Peter's declaration that God is no respecter of persons. The text Pinckney chose for his brief remarks in April 2015 was 2 Samuel 19:1–8. He described this text as a "story about David fighting against his son Absalom" which "he fought with mixed emotions because his country was in the midst of a civil war." While Pinckney did not suggest a moral equivalency between the Union and the Confederacy, he used this biblical story to strike a reconciliatory tone, mourning the deaths of both Union and Confederate soldiers. Invoking Acts 10:34, Pinckney declared, "On this land, even as an African American preacher, I respect and understand that yes Union troops but also Confederate troops fought and *God is not a respecter of persons or causes*. And so we honor all the blood, all the troops, that gave their lives during this time" (emphasis added). Pinckney alludes to Acts

10:34 as a call for a radical reconciliation that acknowledged losses on both sides because God did not favor one soldier over another. One hundred sixty-five years earlier, the author identified as "A Colored American," used the same verse as a warning that God would not save the slaveholding states if the enslaved ever had the means to successfully revolt, because God did not favor one people over another.

Does Acts 10:34 represent an olive branch or a warning? These two different understandings of the implications of this biblical verse for Charleston returns us to the central question that inspired this book. We could ask who interpreted the Bible correctly: Vesey and his fellow conspirators or proslavery apologists like Kennedy, Palmer, Furman, and Dalcho. But perhaps Vesey, his supporters, and even his adversaries were interested in a different and more pressing question. They were not as invested in determining what the Bible means in the abstract as they were in what it implies for the deadly struggle against or the brutal enforcement of American white supremacy. This book has told a story of some early efforts—both hopeful and horrific—to define and control the Bible's implications in the midst of racial terror and violence in an American city. These efforts outlived Vesey in the 1820s, and they outlived "A Colored American" in the 1850s. They continue to this day. On June 17, 2015, less than two months after his reconciliatory sermon in Hampton Park, the Reverend Pinckney was among those murdered by a white supremacist in Emanuel African Methodist Episcopal Church after Pinckney led a Wednesday night Bible study.[11] The enduring but contested question of what the Bible implies in the context of American white supremacy continues to be a matter of life and death in Charleston and cities across this nation.

APPENDIX

The biographical note about Denmark Vesey in Hamilton's *Account*:

As Denmark Vesey has occupied so large a place in the conspiracy, a brief notice of him will, perhaps, be not devoid of interest. The following anecdote will show how near he was to the chance of being distinguished in the bloody events of San Domingo. During the revolutionary war, Captain Vesey, now an old resident of this city, commanded a ship that traded between St. Thomas and Cape Francais (San Domingo.) He was engaged in supplying the French of that Island with Slaves. In the year 1781, he took on board at St. Thomas' 390 slaves and sailed for the Cape; on the passage, he and his officers were struck with the beauty, alertness and intelligence of a boy about 14 years of age, whom they made a pet of, by taking him into the cabin, changing his apparel, and calling him by way of distinction Telemaque, (which appellation has since, by gradual corruption, among the negroes, been changed to Denmark, or sometimes Telmak.) On the arrival, however, of the ship at the Cape, Captain Vesey, having no use for the boy, sold him among his other slaves, and returned to St. Thomas'. On his next voyage to the Cape, he was surprised to learn from his consignee that Telemaque would be returned on his hands, as the planter, who had purchased him, represented him unsound, and subject to epileptic fits. According to the custom of trade in that place, the boy was placed in the hands of the king's physician, who decided that he was unsound, and Captain Vesey was compelled to take him back, of which he had no occasion to repent, as Denmark proved, for 20 years, a most faithful slave. In 1800, Denmark drew a prize of $1500 in the East-Bay-Street Lottery, with which he purchased his freedom from his master, at six hundred dollars, much less than his real value. From that period to the day of his apprehension he has been working as a carpenter in this city, distinguished for great strength and activity. Among his colour he was always looked up to with awe and respect. His temper was impetuous and domineering in the extreme, qualfying [sic] him for the despotic rule, of which he was ambitious. All his passions were ungovernable and savage; and, to his numerous wives and children, he displayed the haughty and capricious cruelty of an Eastern Bashaw. He had nearly effected his escape, after information had been lodged against him. For three days the town was searched for him without success. As early as Monday, the 17th, he had concealed himself. It was not until the night of the 22d of June, during a perfect tempest, that he was found secreted in the house of one of his wives. It is to the uncommon efforts and vigilance of Mr. Wesner, and Capt. Dove, of the City Guard, (the latter of whom seized him) that public justice received its necessary tribute, in the execution of this man. If the party had been one moment later, he would, in all probability, have effected his escape the next day in some outward bound vessel.[1]

Lionel Kennedy's sentence of Denmark Vesey as recorded in Kennedy and Parker's *Official Report*:

Sentence on Denmark Vesey, a Free Black Man.

DENMARK VESEY—The Court, on mature consideration, have pronounced you GUILTY—You have enjoyed the advantage of able Counsel, and were also heard in your own defence, in which you endeavored, with great art and plausibility, to impress a belief of your innocence. After the most patient deliberation, however, the Court were not only satisfied of your guilt, but that you were the author, and original instigator of this diabolical plot. Your professed design was to trample on all laws, human and divine; to riot in blood, outrage, rapine and conflagration, and to introduce anarchy and confusion in their most horrid forms. Your life has become, therefore, a just and necessary sacrifice, at the shrine of indignant Justice. It is difficult to imagine what *infatuation* could have prompted you to attempt an enterprize so wild and visionary. You were a free man; were comparatively wealthy; and enjoyed every comfort, compatible with your situation. You had, therefore, much to risk, and little to gain. From your age and experience, you *ought* to have known, that success was impracticable.

A moments reflection must have convinced you, that the ruin of *your race,* would have been the probable result, and that years' would have rolled away, before they could have recovered that confidence, which, they once enjoyed in this community. The only reparation in your power, is a full disclosure of the truth. In addition to treason, you have committed the grossest impiety, in attempting to pervert the sacred words of God into a sanction for crimes of the blackest hue. It is evident, that you are totally insensible of the divine influence of that Gospel, "all whose paths are peace." It was to reconcile us to our destinies on earth, and to enable us to discharge with fidelity, all the duties of life, that those holy precepts were imparted by Heaven to fallen man.

If you had searched them with sincerity, you would have discovered instructions, immediately applicable to the deluded victims of your artful wiles—"*Servants (says Saint Paul) obey in all things your masters, according to the flesh, not with eye-service, as menpleasers, but in singleness of heart, fearing God.*" And again "*Servants (says Saint Peter) be subject to your masters with all fear, not only to the good and gentle, but also to the forward.*"

On such texts comment is unnecessary.

Your "lamp of life" is nearly extinguished; your race is run; and you must shortly pass "from time to eternity." Let me then conjure you to devote the remnant of your existence in solemn preparation for the awful doom, that awaits you. Your situation is deplorable, but not destitute of spiritual consolation. To that Almighty Being alone, whose Holy Ordinances, you have trampled in the dust, can you now look for mercy, and although "your sins be as scarlet," the tears of sincere penitence may obtain forgiveness at the "Throne of Grace." You cannot have forgotten the history of the malefactor on the Cross, who, like yourself, was the wretched and deluded victim of offended justice. His conscience was awakened in the pangs of dissolution, and yet there is reason to believe, that his spirit was received into the realms of bliss. May *you* imitate his example, and may *your* last moments prove like his![2]

Lionel Kennedy's sentence of (Gullah) Jack Pritchard as recorded in Kennedy and Parker's *Official Report*:

Sentence on Jack, *a Slave belonging to Paul Pritchard, commonly called* GULLAH JACK, *and sometimes* COUTER JACK.

GULLAH JACK—The Court after deliberately considering all the circumstances of your case, are perfectly satisfied of your guilt. In the prosecution of your wicked designs, you were not satisfied with resorting to natural and ordinary means, but endeavoured to enlist on your behalf, all the powers of darkness, and employed for that purpose, the most disgusting mummery and superstition. You represented yourself as invulnerable; that you could neither be taken nor destroyed, and that all who fought under your banners would be invincible. While such wretched expedients are calculated to excite the confidence, or to alarm the fears of the ignorant and credulous, they produce no other emotion in the minds of the intelligent and enlightened, but contempt and disgust. Your boasted charms have not preserved yourself, and of course could not protect others.—

Your Altars and your Gods have sunk together in the dust. The airy spectres, conjured by you, have been chased away by the superior light of Truth, and you stand exposed, the miserable and deluded victim of offended Justice. Your days are literally numbered.

You will shortly be consigned to the cold and silent grave; and all the Powers of Darkness cannot rescue you from your approaching Fate!—Let me then, conjure you to devote the remnant of your miserable existence, in fleeing from the *"wrath to come."* This can only be done by a full disclosure of the truth. The Court are willing to afford you all the aid in their power, and to permit any Minister of the Gospel, whom you may select to have free access to you. To him you may unburthen your guilty conscience. Neglect not the opportunity, for there is "no device nor art in the grave," to which you must shortly be consigned.[3]

Lionel Kennedy's sentence of ten enslaved men collectively as recorded in Kennedy and Parker's *Official Report*:

The Court, on mature deliberation, have pronounced you guilty; the punishment of that guilt is DEATH. Your conduct, on the present occasion, exhibits a degree of depravity and extravigance, rarely paralled. Your professed objects were to trample not only on the laws of this state, but on those of humanity; to commit murder, outrage and plunder, and to substitute for the blessings we enjoy, anarchy and confusion in their most odious forms. The beauties of nature and of art, would have fallen victims to your relentless fury; and even the decripitude of age and the innocence of childhood, would have found no other refuge than the grave!

Surely nothing but infatuation could have prompted you to enter into a plot so wild and diabolical.—A moment's reflection would have convinced you, that disgrace and ruin must have been its consequence, and that it would have probably resulted in the destruction and extermination of *your race*. But if, even complete success had crowned your efforts, what were the golden visions which you anticipated?—Such men as you, are in general, as ignorant as you are vicious, without any settled principles, and possessing but few of the virtues of civilized life; you would soon, therefore, have degenerated into a horde of barbarians, incapable of any government. But admitting that a different result might have taken place, it is natural to enquire, what are the miseries of which you complain?—That we should all earn our bread by the sweat of our brow, is the decree which God pronounced at the fall of man. It extended alike to the master and the slave; to the cottage and the throne. Every one is more or less subject to controul; and the most exalted, as well as the humblest individual, must bow with defference to the laws of that community, in which he is placed by Providence. Your situation, therefore, was neither extraordinary nor unnatural. Servitude has existed under various forms, from the deludge to the present time, and in no age or country has the condition of slaves been milder or more humane than your own. You are, with few exceptions, treated with kindness, and enjoy every comfort compatible with your situation. You are exempt from many of the miseries, to which *the poor* are subject throughout the world. In many countries the life of the slave is at the disposal of his master; here you have always been under the protection of the law.

The tribunal which now imposes this sen[te]nce through its humble organ, affords a strong examplification of the truth of these remarks. In the discharge of the painful duties which have devolved on them the members of this Court have been as anxious to acquit the innocent as determined to condemn the guilty.

In addition to the crime of treason, you have on the present occasion, displayed the vilest ingratitude. It is a melancholy truth, that those servants in whom was reposed the most unlimitted confidence, have been the principal actors in this wicked scheme.

Reared by the hand of kindness, and fostered by a master who assumed many of the duties of a parent—you have realized the fable of the Frozen Serpent, and attempted to destroy the bosom that sheltered and protected you.

You have moreover committed the grossest impiety: you have perverted the sacred words of God, and attempted to torture them into a sanction for crimes, at the bare imagination of which, humanity shudders. Are you incapable of the Heavenly influence of that Gospel, all whose "paths are peace?" It was to reconcile us to our destiny on earth, and to enable us to discharge with fidelity all our duties, whether as master or servant, that those inspired precepts were imparted by Heaven to fallen man.—There is no condition of life which is not embraced by them; and if you had searched them, *in the spirit of truth*, you would have discovered instructions peculiarly applicable to yourselves—

"*Servants (says St. Paul) be obedient to them that are your masters according to the flesh, with fear and trembling, in singleness of your heart, as unto Christ; not with eye-service as men pleasers, but as the servants of Christ, doing the will of God from the heart.*" Had you listened with sincerity to such doctrines, you would not have been arrested by an ignominious death.

Your days on earth are near their close and you now stand upon the confines of eternity. While you linger on this side of the grave, permit me to exhort you, in the name of the everliving God, whose holy ordinances you have violated; to devote most earnestly the remnant of your days, in penitence and preparation for that tribunal, whose sentence, whether pronounced in anger or in mercy, is eternal.

The following were the Negroes on whom the above sentence was pronounced:—Dick, Bacchus, William, Naphur, Adam, Belisle, Charles, Jemmy, Jerry and Dean.[4]

NOTES

Timeline of Major Events

1. For a more detailed timeline, consult Egerton and Paquette, *The Denmark Vesey Affair*, xxix–xlii. Cf. Egerton, *He Shall Go Out Free*, xvii–xx.

Preface

1. Some examples include Fox-Genovese and Genovese, *The Mind of the Master Class*; Oshatz, *Slavery and Sin*; Noll, *The Civil War as a Theological Crisis*; Snay, *Gospel of Disunion*; Stout, *Upon the Altar of the Nation*.

2. Readers interested in these topics should consult the revised and updated version of Egerton's *He Shall Go Out Free*. My reliance on Egerton's work will become apparent throughout this book. Also, Douglas R. Egerton and Robert L. Paquette have recently edited a massive eight hundred–page collection of primary sources titled *The Denmark Vesey Affair: A Documentary History*. This treasure trove of materials updates and greatly expands earlier documentary histories such as John O. Killens's *The Trial Record of Denmark Vesey* (1970), Robert S. Starobin's *Denmark Vesey: The Slave Conspiracy of 1822* (1970), and Edward A. Pearson's *Designs against Charleston: The Trial Record of the Denmark Vesey Slave Conspiracy of 1822* (1999). My quotations from the trial transcripts and several personal letters appear as transcribed in Egerton and Paquette's *The Denmark Vesey Affair*, although, for clarity, I have occasionally altered the punctuation. Although many of the documents in *The Denmark Vesey Affair* appear in abbreviated form, quoting from sources as they appear in Egerton and Paquette's book allows interested readers to check my references against a publically available collection rather than against documents housed in archives or research libraries' special collections that may not be open to the public.

Introduction. Crimes of the Blackest Hue

1. Hamilton, *An Account of the Late Intended Insurrection among a Portion of the Blacks of This City*, 41. In their *Official Report*, Lionel Henry Kennedy and Thomas Parker, the magistrates at Jack Purcell's trial, claimed that he made this statement in

a confession to James Hamilton, the intendant (or mayor) of Charleston, moments before his death. Kennedy and Parker wrote, "THE COURT *unanimously* found Jack GUILTY, and passed upon him the sentence of Death.—A few moments preceding his execution, he made the following CONFESSION to the Intendant of Charleston" (quoted in Egerton and Paquette, *The Denmark Vesey Affair*, 214; emphasis in the original). All quotations from the *Official Report* in this book come from the transcription in Egerton and Paquette, *The Denmark Vesey Affair*.

2. In 1804, rebels declared independence in Haiti, and by 1822, the Haitian government was encouraging the migration of people of African descent to the island. Recently, scholars have debated the scope and details of the 1822 insurrection plot in Charleston. A few have presented it as a false accusation started by Hamilton to set up Vesey and his associates. Yet, for good reason, this position has not convinced many historians. While the extensive testimonies by enslaved people were in all likelihood coerced, it does not mean that they were fabricated. Moreover, private letters written by Mary Lamboll Beach and Martha Proctor Richardson a few days after Vesey's death dovetail with details within the trial transcripts published later that year. For recent debates over the historical accuracy of this source material, consult Egerton, *He Shall Go Out Free*, 253–60; Egerton and Paquette, *The Denmark Vesey Affair*, xxi–xxiv; L. Ford, "An Interpretation of the Denmark Vesey Insurrection Scare," 7–22; Gross, "Forum: The Making of a Slave Conspiracy, Part 2," 135–202; M. Johnson, "Denmark Vesey and His Co-conspirators," 915–76; Paquette and Egerton, "Of Facts and Fables," 8–48; Spady, "Power and Confession," 287–304; and Wade, "The Vesey Plot," 143–61.

3. Hamilton, *An Account*, 27. Kennedy and Parker offer a slightly different number of those convicted but not executed. They claim, "The whole number arrested were one hundred and thirty one, of whom sixty-seven were convicted.—From amongst those convicted, thirty-five were executed; the remainder will be sent beyond the limits of the United States" (Egerton and Paquette, *The Denmark Vesey Affair*, 86). Kennedy and Parker's number agrees with the number provided by Governor Thomas Bennett Jr. In a lengthy circular dated August 10, 1822, he wrote "the whole number, seventy-two, have been disposed of; thirty-five executed, and thirty-seven sentenced to banishment" (Egerton and Paquette, *The Denmark Vesey Affair*, 469). None of these sources include the four men identified as "white" (William Allen, Jacob Danders, John Igneshias, and Andrew S. Rhodes) convicted on the charge of "a Misdemeanor in inciting Slaves to Insurrection" on October 7, 1822, by Judge Elihu Hall Bay (Egerton and Paquette, *The Denmark Vesey Affair*, 270–76). The court noted that there was no solid evidence that these four men were actually involved in Vesey's plot.

4. Egerton and Paquette, *The Denmark Vesey Affair*, 418.

5. In Judges 13:5, an angel tells Samson's mother, "he shall begin to deliver Israel out of the hand of the Philistines." Samson dies in his struggle with the Philistines when he destroys their temple. Some biblical texts describe God or David as delivering the Israelites from "the hand of the Philistines" (e.g., 1 Samuel 7:3; 2 Samuel 19:9 [v. 10 in Hebrew]). Nevertheless, Beach probably alludes to Samson, because immediately after this reference she suggests that Vesey understood his death as a type of martyrdom, which is a common interpretation of Samson's death. Elsewhere in antebellum literature, references to Samson's death in the Philistine temple were used to describe militant opponents of slavery as martyrs for the antislavery cause. Consult Junior and Schipper, *Black Samson*, 4–5. In his 1972 biography of Vesey written for young adults, John Oliver Killens quotes lyrics from a song about Samson when he imagines the reaction of others to Vesey's preaching. While describing Vesey's sermon, Killen writes, "One of the brothers began to sing a Negro spiritual. Others joined him, humming softly: 'If I hadda my way, If I hadda my way, little chillun, I'd bring this building down'" (Killens, *Great Gittin' Up Morning*, 62). These lyrics come from the chorus of a song about Samson that refers to his destruction of the Philistine temple, during which he killed himself and three thousand Philistines in the process (Judges 16:23–30). For the lyrics and discussion of this song within African American art and literature, consult Junior and Schipper, *Black Samson*, 58–61.

6. Egerton and Paquette, *The Denmark Vesey Affair*, 376; emphasis in the original.

7. Egerton and Paquette, *The Denmark Vesey Affair*, 378; emphasis in the original. Beach does not identify the specific psalms that were allegedly sung or indicate whether they were actually spirituals rather than biblical psalms. Documents related to earlier slave revolts also indicate that prisoners sang religious songs the night before their executions. In 1800, an enslaved blacksmith named Gabriel organized a revolt near Richmond, Virginia. The plot was suppressed before it could be carried out, and over two dozen enslaved people were executed, including Gabriel. In a letter, dated September 11, 1800, to Virginia governor James Monroe, who later became the president of the United States, William Rose wrote that the night before the first executions of men accused of participating in Gabriel's plot "the whole Jail was alive with Hymns of Praise to the Great God and here (I hope) penitence instantly began." For Rose's entire letter to Monroe, consult Schwarz, *Gabriel's Conspiracy*, 36. In chapter 3, I discuss how slaveholders involved in Vesey's case had an alleged concern that the condemned parties repent and save their souls before they died.

8. Egerton and Paquette, *The Denmark Vesey Affair*, 166; emphasis in the original.

9. African American literature includes many examples of connections between the United States and Egypt as depicted in the Bible. For detailed studies, consult,

among others, Callahan, *The Talking Bible*; Coffey, *Exodus and Liberation*, 79–177; Glaude, *Exodus!*, 44–62; Marbury, *Pillars of Cloud and Fire*; Powery and Sadler, *The Genesis of Liberation*; Raboteau, "African Americans, Exodus and American Israel," 1–17; T. Smith, *Conjuring Culture*, 55–80; and Thomas, *Claiming Exodus*.

10. Egerton and Paquette, *The Denmark Vesey Affair*, 178.

11. Egerton and Paquette, *The Denmark Vesey Affair*, 181.

12. Egerton and Paquette, *The Denmark Vesey Affair*, 181.

13. Hamilton, *An Account*, 25.

14. Egerton and Paquette, *The Denmark Vesey Affair*, 224.

15. Egerton and Paquette, *The Denmark Vesey Affair*, 224.

16. Egerton and Paquette, *The Denmark Vesey Affair*, 212.

17. Grimké, *Right on the Scaffold*.

18. Grimké, *Right on the Scaffold*, 12.

19. Bailey, *Biographical Directory of the South Carolina House of Representatives*, 4:329–30.

20. Egerton and Paquette, *The Denmark Vesey Affair*, 162.

21. Egerton and Paquette, *The Denmark Vesey Affair*, 184–85.

22. Egerton and Paquette, *The Denmark Vesey Affair*, 78–79; emphasis in the original.

23. Egerton and Paquette, *The Denmark Vesey Affair*, 299.

24. Egerton and Paquette, *The Denmark Vesey Affair*, 234.

25. Egerton and Paquette, *The Denmark Vesey Affair*, 750. Child's letter to Higginson served as one of the sources for Higginson's 1861 article on Vesey in the *Atlantic Monthly*, which I discuss later in this chapter.

26. Stowe, *Dred: A Tale of the Great Dismal Swamp*, 1:253–54, 2:214.

27. Hamilton, *An Account*. Hamilton signed the preface on the first page and dated it August 16, 1822.

28. Although the *Official Report* and *An Account* differ in length, they tend to agree in content when describing the same events (Egerton and Paquette, *The Denmark Vesey Affair*, xvii).

29. All quotations from "Evidence Document B" in this book come from the transcription in Egerton and Paquette, *The Denmark Vesey Affair*.

30. Egerton and Paquette, *The Denmark Vesey Affair*, xvii.

31. Bibb, *Slave Insurrection in 1831*, 5.

32. Grimké, *Right on the Scaffold*, 3–6. Egerton suggests that the material on Vesey's early life in Grimké's work that does not come from Hamilton's pamphlet may have come from African American residents of Charleston and the prominent white abolitionist Angela Grimké, who, raised in the family that enslaved Archibald, was also living in Charleston in 1822 (Egerton, *He Shall Go Out Free*, 253–54).

33. Brawley, *A Short History of the American Negro*, 93–95; DuBois, *The Negro Church*, 23–24.

34. Egerton, *He Shall Go Out Free*, 20.

35. Quoted in Egerton and Paquette, *The Denmark Vesey Affair*, 10.

36. For an analysis of Vesey's plot and its aftermath that, among other things, discusses white Charlestonians' fears that the ability of enslaved and free Black residents to work on their own and to keep some or all of their wages could foment insurrection and threaten an economy built on slavery, consult Hill Edwards, *Unfree Markets*, 102–24.

37. Hamilton, *An Account*, 15. For the same identification in the *Official Report*, consult Egerton and Paquette, *The Denmark Vesey Affair*, 181, 184.

38. The description appears in a letter from Lydia Maria Child to Thomas Wentworth Higginson, dated March 17, 1860. She implies, however, that her conversation with Thomas Cilavan Brown, which she recorded in a journal, occurred decades earlier.

39. Egerton and Paquette, *The Denmark Vesey Affair*, 3.

40. Simms, *The History of South Carolina*, 328.

41. Egerton and Paquette, *The Denmark Vesey Affair*, 184; emphasis in the original.

42. Egerton and Paquette, *The Denmark Vesey Affair*, 190–91; cf. 335–36. Hamilton places Gell's first confession on July 13 (*An Account*, 20) and mentions that Monday's list consisted of forty-two names "every one of whom have been apprehended" (27–28). Hamilton provides additional background information on Monday Gell in a lengthy note on the bottom of pp. 20–21.

43. Egerton and Paquette, *The Denmark Vesey Affair*, 214; emphasis in the original.

44. Egerton and Paquette, *The Denmark Vesey Affair*, 75.

45. Although suspected, Morris Brown and Henry Drayton were not convicted of involvement in Vesey's conspiracy. Hamilton concluded that "after the most diligent search and scrutiny, no evidence entitled to belief, has been discovered against them. A hearsay rumour, in relation to *Morris Brown*, was traced far enough to end in its complete falsification" (Hamilton, *An Account*, 28–29; emphasis in the original). It appears that Vesey and his associates did not trust Morris Brown and the leadership of the African Church. According to one of Monday Gell's confessions, "Morris Brown, Harry Drayton and Charles Corr, and other influential leaders of the African Church were never consulted on this subject for fear they would betray us to the Whites" (Egerton and Paquette, *The Denmark Vesey Affair*, 192). Later generations would attribute the betrayal of Vesey to tensions between mixed race and Black Charlestonians. For example, according to an article in the *New York Tribune*, Martin Robison Delany, an African American medical doctor who achieved the rank of

major during the Civil War, gave a speech on May 12, 1865, at Zion Presbyterian Church in Charleston in which he "sought to show that the ill-feeling between the blacks and mulattoes arose out of the betrayal of Denmark Vesey by a mulatto!" (quoted in Egerton and Paquette, *The Denmark Vesey Affair*, 771).

46. James Osgood Andrew, "Letters on Methodist History," 24. For a more recent overview of the Methodist Church in Charleston in the years leading up to Vesey's plot, consult Hinks, *To Awaken My Afflicted Brethren*, 22–28.

47. Petition of the Inhabitants of Charleston, October 16, 1820, Petitions to the General Assembly, no. 143, series S165015, South Carolina Department of Archives and History. Quoted in Egerton and Paquette, *The Denmark Vesey Affair*, 56; emphasis in the original. For a list of signatures on the petition, consult Egerton and Paquette, *The Denmark Vesey Affair*, 56–58.

48. Egerton and Paquette, *The Denmark Vesey Affair*, 135.

49. Quoted in Paquette and Egerton, "Of Facts and Fables," 41. Richard Furman would reiterate this position a few months later in a letter to South Carolina's new governor, John L. Wilson, dated December 24, 1822, but published the following year in an influential pamphlet, which I discuss in detail in chapter 5, titled *Exposition of the Views of the Baptists, Relative to the Coloured Population of the United States*. Furman claimed that a "considerable number of those who were found guilty and executed, laid claim to a religious character; yet several of these were grossly immoral, and, in general, they were members of an irregular body, which called itself the *African Church*, and had intimate connection and intercourse with a similar body of men in a Northern City, among whom the supposed right to emancipation is strenuously advocated" (17; emphasis in the original).

50. Henry, "The Police Control of the Slave in South Carolina," 138.

51. Hamilton, *An Account*, 29; emphasis in the original.

52. Egerton and Paquette, *The Denmark Vesey Affair*, 77.

53. Although Richardson was not living in Charleston at the time, her information came indirectly from Hamilton. Consult Paquette, "From Rebellion to Revisionism," 314–17.

54. Egerton and Paquette, *The Denmark Vesey Affair*, 77.

55. Egerton and Paquette, *The Denmark Vesey Affair*, 77. Charles, who was enslaved by the widow of Thomas Shubrick, a planter who enslaved over 250 people at the time of his death, was acquitted. But Peter Poyas, who was enslaved by James Poyas, and Ned Bennett, who was enslaved by Governor Thomas Bennett, were among those hanged with Vesey on July 2.

56. Hamilton, *An Account*, 29. Just over a week after Brown and Drayton's trial and banishment, an advertisement in the August 14, 1822, edition of the *Charleston Courier* reads, "On Friday afternoon, at four o'clock, will be sold by the order of the

Trustees of the African Church, on their Lot in Hampstead, All the Lumber, Which comprised the said Church, in lots to suit purchasers" (Egerton and Paquette, *The Denmark Vesey Affair*, 667). From this advertisement, Egerton and Paquette conclude that the church had not burned down, as popularly rumored, but was dismantled and sold off for lumber.

57. Egerton and Paquette, *The Denmark Vesey Affair*, 667.

58. Hamilton, *An Account*, 4.

59. Hamilton, *An Account*, 4.

60. Hamilton, *An Account*, 4.

61. Hamilton, *An Account*, 20–21.

62. Egerton and Paquette, *The Denmark Vesey Affair*, 192; emphasis in the original.

63. Egerton and Paquette, *The Denmark Vesey Affair*, 198.

64. Stowe, *Dred: A Tale of the Great Dismal Swamp*, 1:250.

65. Higginson, "Denmark Vesey," 728–44. Higginson's article served as a source for Williams's brief discussion of Vesey in his *History of the Negro Race in America from 1619 to 1881*, 2:84–85. Williams was a Civil War veteran, historian, Baptist minister, and member of the Ohio state legislature.

66. Grimké, *Right on the Scaffold*, 12.

67. Grimké, *Right on the Scaffold*, 12. Both the spellings "Zechariah" and "Zachariah" occur in Kennedy and Parker's documents.

68. Egerton and Paquette, *The Denmark Vesey Affair*, 326; emphasis in the original.

69. Egerton and Paquette, *The Denmark Vesey Affair*, 213.

70. Egerton, "'Why They Did Not Preach Up This Thing,'" 298–318.

71. Egerton and Paquette, *The Denmark Vesey Affair*, 261; emphasis in the original.

72. Dalcho, *Practical Considerations Founded on the Scriptures*, 33. Dalcho refers specifically to John 14:1–3, in which Jesus says, "Let not your heart be troubled: ye believe in God, believe also in me. In my Father's house are many mansions: if it were not so, I would have told you. I go to prepare a place for you. And if I go and prepare a place for you, I will come again, and receive you unto myself; that where I am, there ye may be also."

73. Egerton and Paquette, *The Denmark Vesey Affair*, 83.

74. This may be because religious practices among people of African descent in South Carolina were different from those of people of African descent in Virginia when Gabriel organized his suppressed revolt against slaveholders in 1800 or when Nat Turner organized his revolt in 1831, although Gabriel, Vesey, Turner, and their respective associates all appealed to the Bible to some extent. For a succinct discussion

of the different religious contexts that shaped Gabriel, Vesey, and Turner's respective plots that challenges scholarly opinion that presents the religious practices of the enslaved in the United States as if they were monolithic, consult Sidbury, "Reading, Revelation, and Rebellion," 119–33.

75. Egerton and Paquette, *The Denmark Vesey Affair*, 164.

76. Egerton and Paquette, *The Denmark Vesey Affair*, 77.

77. Washington, "The Meaning of Scripture in Gullah Concepts of Liberation and Group Identity," 332. For a general introduction to Gullah religion and medicine, consult Cross, *Gullah Culture in America*, 86–123.

78. Genovese, *Roll, Jordan, Roll*, 594.

79. On Philip as a conjurer who utilized traditional African religious practices as well as biblical texts, consult Rucker, *The River Flows On*, 167–68.

80. Grimké, *Right on the Scaffold*, 3.

81. Grimké, *Right on the Scaffold*, 4, 6, 7, 10.

82. Some of the many examples from the nineteenth century include the writings of Hanna Crafts, Fredrick Douglass, and John Jea. Consult Bassard, *Transforming Scriptures*, 20–21, 70.

83. Although there is no reference to this specific verse in the trial transcripts, there are multiple references to the biblical chapter in which this verse appears (Exodus 21) as well as the book of Exodus in general.

Chapter One. He Shall Surely Be Put to Death

1. Bourne, *The Book and Slavery Irreconcilable with Animadversions upon Dr. Smith's Philosophy*.

2. In the King James Version, 1 Timothy 1:9–11 reads, "Knowing this, that the law is not made for a righteous man, but for the lawless and disobedient, for the ungodly and for sinners, for unholy and profane, for murderers of fathers and murderers of mothers, for manslayers, For whoremongers, for them that defile themselves with mankind, for *menstealers*, for liars, for perjured persons, and if there be any other thing that is contrary to sound doctrine; According to the glorious gospel of the blessed God, which was committed to my trust" (emphasis added).

3. Quoted in Bourne, *The Book and Slavery Irreconcilable*, 29.

4. Quoted in Bourne, *The Book and Slavery Irreconcilable*, 25; emphasis in the original. Immediately after quoting Clarke's commentary on Exodus 21:16, Bourne turns to a similar law found in Deuteronomy 24:7: "*If a man be found stealing any of his brethren of the children of Israel and maketh merchandize of him, or sellth him, then that THIEF shall die*" (Bourne, *The Book and Slavery Irreconcilable*, 26; emphasis in the original). A key difference between this verse and Exodus 21:16 is that Deuteronomy narrows its condemnation to only cases involving the stealing of Israelites.

One could object that this verse would not apply to the transatlantic slave trade because it does not involve the stealing of Israelites. In anticipation of this objection, Bourne included a lengthy passage by Thomas Scott, an Anglican priest who was well known at the time for his *Commentary on the Whole Bible*. Begun in 1788, Scott's commentary sold widely in England and United States. On Deuteronomy 24:7, Scott argued that this text is applicable beyond ancient Israel because "Christianity has annihilated that distinction of nations which was once established; every man is now our brother, whatever his nation complexion or creed" (cf. Galatians 3:28) (quoted in Bourne, *The Book and Slavery Irreconcilable*, 26). By this logic, Deuteronomy 24:7 would still apply to any Christian involved in the slave trade. As discussed later in this chapter, in *Thoughts and Sentiments on the Evil and Wicked Traffic of the Slavery*, Ottobah Cugoano combined Deuteronomy 24:7 and Exodus 21:16 in his book's epigraph but did not include the reference to "his brethren of the children of Israel," thereby giving his antislavery epigraph a more universal application.

5. *Old South Leaflets*, 7:274.

6. Bradford and Moore, "The First Printed Protest against Slavery in America," 267; emphasis in the original.

7. Sewall, *The Selling of Joseph*, 1; emphasis in the original.

8. Crèvecoeur, *Letters from an American Farmer*.

9. Although the letters are fictitious, Crèvecoeur traveled though the Carolinas, and he may have based some of the events in the letters on his own experiences during his journeys.

10. "Extract from 'Letters from an American Farmer' by J. Hector St. John, a Farmer in Pennsylvania," 209–11.

11. Introduction to "Extract from 'Letters from an American Farmer,'" 209.

12. Cugoano, *Thoughts and Sentiments*, 1; emphasis in the original. Unless otherwise indicated, all quotations of this work are from the 1787 edition.

13. Although Cugoano quotes biblical texts quite frequently, he does not always identify quotations of an individual text or combinations of different biblical texts by chapter and verse. For example, in the opening pages he declares, "Black People have been so unjustly deprived, cannot fail in meeting with the applause of all good men, and the approbation of that which will for ever redound to their honor; they have the warrant of that which is divine: *Open thy mouth, judge righteously, plead the cause of the poor and needy* [Proverbs 31:9]; *for the liberal deviseth liberal things, and by liberal things shall stand* [Isaiah 32:8]" (Cugoano, *Thoughts and Sentiments*, 2; emphasis in the original). Later, he writes that Christians are "*commanded to cast off the works of darkness, and to put on the whole armour of righteousness and light* [Romans 13:12]; *and that they may be strong in the Lord, and in the power of his might* [Ephesians 6:10]" (Cugoano, *Thoughts and Sentiments*, 52; emphasis in the original).

14. Edwards (the younger), *The Injustice and Impolicy of the Slave Trade*, 30.

15. Edwards (the younger), *The Injustice and Impolicy of the Slave Trade*, 30.

16. Booth, *Commerce in the Human Species*, 6.

17. Booth, *Commerce in the Human Species*, 7; emphasis in the original.

18. Hamilton, *An Account*, 26.

19. The Petition of Joseph L. Enslow, Thursday, December 1, 1831. Quoted in Egerton and Paquette, *The Denmark Vesey Affair*, 638.

20. Egerton and Paquette, *The Denmark Vesey Affair*, 326; emphasis in the original. Cf. Egerton, *He Shall Go Out Free*, 114. The transcription of John Enslow's second confession, which only appears in "Evidence Document B," also cites the other passages as the biblical texts and lessons used at the meeting: "Text. Zachariah 14. 1–2 . . . Lessons, Exodus/Chapter—Isaiah 19–20 chapters" (Egerton and Paquette, *The Denmark Vesey Affair*, 326–27). I discuss the relevance of these biblical texts for Vesey's plot later in this chapter.

21. The Petition of Joseph L. Enslow, Thursday, December 1, 1831. Quoted in Egerton and Paquette, *The Denmark Vesey Affair*, 638.

22. Egerton and Paquette, *The Denmark Vesey Affair*, 74–75.

23. Egerton and Paquette, *The Denmark Vesey Affair*, 377; emphasis in the original. Beach admits that Vesey is correct but condescendingly claims that they created a separate catechism to "accommodate," as she put it, the text to the understanding of people of African descent rather than to conceal certain biblical texts from them.

24. Egerton and Paquette, *The Denmark Vesey Affair*, 323. This testimony is not included in the *Official Report* but appears in "Evidence Document B."

25. Egerton and Paquette, *The Denmark Vesey Affair*, 323. Most likely, Kennedy and Parker's identification of the texts to which Bacchus alludes comes from the testimony of John Enslow, discussed earlier in this chapter (cf. n. 19 of this chapter).

26. Kennedy and Parker mistakenly write "utter destroyed" instead of "utterly destroyed" as it appears in the King James Version. This verse could be interpreted as verifying the Israelites' obedience to a divine command regarding the treatment of certain cities in Canaan. According to Deuteronomy 20:16, God commanded the Israelites, "But of the cities of these people, which the LORD thy God doth give thee for an inheritance, thou shalt save alive nothing that breatheth."

27. Robertson, *Denmark Vesey*, 138.

28. Similarly, journalist John Lofton lists Colossians 4:1 and Exodus 2:23–24 as texts that "could be adopted to the cause of Negro freedom," although there is no extant evidence that Vesey or his associates appealed to these passages (Lofton, *Insurrection in South Carolina*, 133). In addition to texts mentioned in the court documents, Killens has Vesey quote Mark 1:17 when he imagines what a sermon by Vesey might have been like (Killens, *Great Gittin' Up Morning*, 62–63).

29. Hamilton, *An Account*, 33; emphasis in the original. This confession was also published in the Hartford *Connecticut Mirror* on September 16, 1822. The versions of

this confession in the *Official Report* and "Evidence Document B" contain only minor differences in punctuation. Cf. Egerton and Paquette, *The Denmark Vesey Affair*, 166, 295, respectively. The version in "Evidence Document B" does not contain the parenthetical specification of the insurrection's date as June 16.

30. Hamilton, *An Account*, 38. The version of this confession in the *Official Report* contains only minor differences in punctuation. Cf. Egerton and Paquette, *The Denmark Vesey Affair*, 178.

31. Egerton and Paquette, *The Denmark Vesey Affair*, 166–67; emphasis in the original. The *Official Report* does not identify the specific psalms to which Rolla refers or whether they were the same psalms that Beach mentions in her letter, discussed in the introduction.

32. The 1820 petition to the South Carolina legislature calling for further restrictions on people of African descent, which I discussed in the previous chapter, includes "B Elliott" (presumably Benjamin Elliott) among its signatures. According to the 1830 federal census, Elliott enslaved sixteen people.

33. After graduating from Princeton, then known as the College of New Jersey, in 1806, Elliott returned to Charleston and practiced law in the offices of Thomas Parker. Along with Kennedy, Elliott represented St. Philip and St. Michael parishes in the twenty-first General Assembly of the South Carolina House of Representatives in 1814–15 (Bailey, *Biographical Directory of the South Carolina House of Representatives*, 4:182, 329–30).

34. For the full text of Elliott's article, consult Egerton and Paquette, *The Denmark Vesey Affair*, 502–5.

35. Egerton and Paquette, *The Denmark Vesey Affair*, 503; emphasis in the original.

36. Egerton and Paquette, *The Denmark Vesey Affair*, 503; emphasis in the original.

37. A longer account of the Israelites' battles with Og and Sihon appears in Numbers 21:25–35. Yet the reference to "sixty cities" that Elliott cites occurs only in the account in Deuteronomy 3.

38. In its entirety, Numbers 31:7–18 reads, "And they warred against the Midianites, as the LORD commanded Moses; and they slew all the males. And they slew the kings of Midian, beside the rest of them that were slain; namely, Evi, and Rekem, and Zur, and Hur, and Reba, five kings of Midian: Balaam also the son of Beor they slew with the sword. And the children of Israel took all the women of Midian captives, and their little ones, and took the spoil of all their cattle, and all their flocks, and all their goods. And they burnt all their cities wherein they dwelt, and all their goodly castles, with fire. And they took all the spoil, and all the prey, both of men and of beasts. And they brought the captives, and the prey, and the spoil, unto Moses, and Eleazar the priest, and unto the congregation of the children of Israel, unto the

camp at the plains of Moab, which are by Jordan near Jericho. And Moses, and Eleazar the priest, and all the princes of the congregation, went forth to meet them without the camp. And Moses was wroth with the officers of the host, with the captains
over thousands, and captains over hundreds, which came from the battle. And Moses
said unto them, Have ye saved all the women alive? Behold, these caused the children
of Israel, through the counsel of Balaam, to commit trespass against the LORD in
the matter of Peor, and there was a plague among the congregation of the LORD.
Now therefore kill every male among the little ones, and kill every woman that hath
known man by lying with him. But all the women children, that have not known a
man by lying with him, keep alive for yourselves."

39. "And David and his men went up, and invaded the Geshurites, and the Gez-
rites, and the Amalekites: for those nations were of old the inhabitants of the land,
as thou goest to Shur, even unto the land of Egypt. And David smote the land, and
left neither man nor woman alive, and took away the sheep, and the oxen, and the
asses, and the camels, and the apparel" (1 Samuel 27:8–9). The translation of these
verses in the King James Version follows the standard Hebrew text, although some
Greek manuscripts may have been a translation of an earlier Hebrew version of these
verses. For further discussion of these differences in the Hebrew and Greek manuscripts, consult McCarter, 1 Samuel: A New Translation with Introduction and Commentary, 413.

40. Vesey was not the first person involved in an insurrection plot against slavery
in the United States to imply a connection between white slaveholders and the Canaanites or inhabitants of nearby lands. One finds a similar identification between
the white slaveholding residents of Richmond, Virginia, and the inhabitants living
in or around Canaan implied in the court records related to the suppressed insurrection plot by an enslaved man named Gabriel in 1800. According to the testimony of
an enslaved man named Ben Woolfolk, Gabriel's brother Martin argued that God
endorsed their plan by paraphrasing part of Leviticus 26:8 as, "five of you shall conquer an hundred & a hundred a thousand of our enemies." Leviticus 26 promises that
the Israelites will defeat their enemies from around Canaan, and Martin implicitly
associates these peoples with the white slaveholding residents of Richmond. For
Martin's paraphrase of Leviticus 26:8, consult Schwarz, Gabriel's Conspiracy, 70.

41. Brown, The Black Man, 143.

42. Egerton and Paquette, The Denmark Vesey Affair, 296.

43. Egerton and Paquette, The Denmark Vesey Affair, 324; emphasis in the original.
This testimony is not included in the Official Report but appears in "Evidence
Document B."

44. In a brief discussion of Denmark Vesey, Seth Perry, a historian of American
religion at Princeton University, refers to this type of interaction with the Bible as
"performed Biblicism," a term he uses for "biblical identifications predicated on ac-

tion for their application and recognition" (Perry, *Bible Culture and Authority in the Early United States*, 67).

Chapter Two. By the Mouth of Witnesses

1. Reprinted in Egerton and Paquette, *The Denmark Vesey Affair*, 131–34.

2. Examples include the July 8, 1822, issue of the Hartford-based *Connecticut Mirror*; the July 9, 1822, issue of the Philadelphia-based *United States Gazette and True American*; the July 10, 1822, issue of the Washington, DC–based *National Intelligencer*; the July 10, 1822, issue of the Philadelphia-based *National Gazette and Literary Register*; the July 15, 1822, issue of the Salem, MA–based *Gazette*; and the July 31, 1822, issue of the Louisville-based *Public Advertiser* (Egerton and Paquette, *The Denmark Vesey Affair*, 134n5).

3. Egerton and Paquette, *The Denmark Vesey Affair*, 132.

4. Egerton and Paquette, *The Denmark Vesey Affair*, 132.

5. Egerton and Paquette, *The Denmark Vesey Affair*, 133.

6. Egerton and Paquette, *The Denmark Vesey Affair*, 133.

7. Reprinted in Egerton and Paquette, *The Denmark Vesey Affair*, 134.

8. Egerton and Paquette, *The Denmark Vesey Affair*, 417.

9. Quoted in the preface to Hamilton, *An Account*, 2.

10. Hamilton, *An Account*, 2.

11. Hamilton, *An Account*, 12.

12. For a history of the Stono rebellion, consult Hoffer, *Cry Liberty: The Great Stono River Slave Rebellion of 1739*. For a collection of historical documents and essays related to the rebellion, consult M. Smith, *Stono: Documenting and Interpreting a Southern Slave Revolt*.

13. Egerton and Paquette, *The Denmark Vesey Affair*, 214, 225, 312, 317. According to Hamilton, Lot "was the *courier* of the conspiracy, and was proved to have gone out of town, for the purpose of inducing the country negroes to join in the insurrection" (Hamilton, *An Account*, 24; emphasis in the original). Lot was among the twenty-two enslaved persons hanged on July 26, 1822.

14. Hamilton, *An Account*, 30; emphasis in the original.

15. The relevant portion of the 1805 Act for the Punishment of Certain Crimes against the State of South-Carolina reads, "*Be it enacted, by the honorable the Senate and House of Representatives, now met and sitting in General Assembly, and by the authority of the same,* That from and immediately after the passing of this Act, every person or persons, who shall, or may be, either directly or indirectly, concerned or connected with any slave or slaves, in a state of actual insurrection within this state; or who shall, in any manner, or to any extent, excite, counsel, advise, induce, aid, comfort or assist, any slave or slaves, to raise, or attempt to raise an insurrection

within this state, by furnishing them with any written or other passport, with any arms or ammunition, or munition of war, or knowing of their assembling for any purpose tending to treason or insurrection, shall afford to them shelter or protection, or shall permit his, her, or their house, or houses, to be resorted to by any slave or slaves, for any purpose tending to treason or insurrection, as aforesaid, shall on conviction thereof in any court having jurisdiction thereof, by confession in open court, or by the testimony of two witnesses, be adjudged guilty of treason against the state, and suffer Death" (*Acts and Resolutions of the General Assembly of the State of South-Carolina, Passed in December, 1805*, 49–50; emphasis in the original).

16. Hamilton, *An Account*, 12.

17. Hamilton, *An Account*, 12. Kennedy and Parker's introductory narrative to their *Official Report* includes these three rules, with slight differences in wording, plus two others. Kennedy and Parker write, "The Court however, determined to adopt those rules, whenever they were not repugnant to, nor expressly excepted by that statute, nor inconsistent with the local situation and policy of the state; and laid down for their own government the following regulations:—First—That no slave should be tried, except in the presence of his owner, or his counsel, and that notice should be given, in every case, at least one day before the trial: Second—That the testimony of one witness, unsupported by additional evidence, or by circumstances, should lead to no conviction of a *capital* nature: Third—That the witnesses should be confronted with the accused, and with each other, in every case, except where testimony was given under a solemn pledge that the names of the witnesses should not be divulged, as they declared in some instances, that they apprehended being murdered by the blacks, if it was known that they had volunteered their evidence: Fourth—That the prisoners might be represented by counsel, whenever this was requested by the owners of the slaves, or by the prisoners themselves, if free: Fifth—That the statements or defences of the accused should be heard, in every case, and they be permitted themselves to examine any witness they thought proper" (Egerton and Paquette, *The Denmark Vesey Affair*, 159; emphasis in the original).

18. Hamilton, *An Account*, 12.

19. Hamilton, *An Account*, 12–13; parenthetical material in the original.

20. Egerton and Paquette, *The Denmark Vesey Affair*, 169.

21. Hamilton, *An Account*, 13; parenthetical material in the original.

22. Hamilton, *An Account*, 13.

23. Hamilton, *An Account*, 14.

24. Hamilton, *An Account*, 14; emphasis added.

25. Hamilton, *An Account*, 14.

26. Egerton and Paquette, *The Denmark Vesey Affair*, 171.

27. Egerton and Paquette, *The Denmark Vesey Affair*, 175.

28. Hamilton, *An Account*, 14; emphasis in the original.

29. Hamilton, *An Account*, 15.

30. Hamilton, *An Account*, 15–16.

31. Hamilton, *An Account*, 16.

32. Hamilton, *An Account*, 16.

33. Hamilton, *An Account*, 16.

34. Egerton and Paquette, *The Denmark Vesey Affair*, 184. The phrase "bearing false witness against him" may be an allusion to the King James Version's rendering of the ninth commandment: "Thou shalt not bear false witness against thy neighbor" (Exodus 20:16; Deuteronomy 5:20).

35. Egerton and Paquette, *The Denmark Vesey Affair*, 177.

36. Hamilton, *An Account*, 17.

37. Hamilton, *An Account*, 17; emphasis added.

38. For example, Hamilton groups together the investigation and executions "of John Horry, Harry Haig and Gullah Jack," writing, "for the guilt of the latter, see Appendix (D.)(E.)&(F.)" (Hamilton, *An Account*, 19).

39. Hamilton, *An Account*, 18. Jesse and Rolla's confessions were discussed in the previous chapter.

40. Egerton and Paquette, *The Denmark Vesey Affair*, 378. For the full text of this letter, consult Egerton and Paquette, *The Denmark Vesey Affair*, 376–79.

41. *Old South Leaflets*, 7:267.

42. *Acts and Resolutions of the General Assembly of the State of South-Carolina*, 50. In July 1817, local Baptists drafted a one-page document titled "Rules and Regulations for the Coloured Ministers, Elders, and Members of the Baptists Church, in Charleston, S. C." The seventh regulation states, "An accusation against an Elder, according to the express words of Scripture, is not to be received but before (or on the testimony of) two or three witnesses." In this case, however, the "express words of Scripture" refer to 1 Timothy 5:19 ("Against an elder receive not an accusation, but before two or three witnesses") rather than the laws about the number of witnesses required in cases involving murder or capital punishment in Numbers and Deuteronomy.

43. Hamilton, *An Account*, 15. Daniel 6:27 refers to God as the one "who hath delivered Daniel from the power of the lions." On June 26, 1822, the court concluded that the letter on its own was not sufficient evidence to find Abraham guilty. "Although this letter was extremely suspicious," Hamilton wrote, "there being no other testimony against Abraham, he was found *not guilty*" (Hamilton, *An Account*, 15; emphasis in the original). Hamilton includes the court's verdict as if to show that it strictly followed the guideline about the need for multiple witnesses to warrant a verdict of capital punishment.

44. After quoting Kennedy's rulings, Hamilton explains, "The above Sentences is selected out of the many passed on this occasion, with a view, to give the reader a general idea of them" (Hamilton, *An Account*, 48).

45. These men were all hanged on July 26, 1822, except for William Paul, who was banished under penalty of death if he returned.

46. On Vesey's performance of recognizably biblical roles, consult Perry, *Bible Culture and Authority in the Early United States*, 65–67. Perry, however, does not discuss Hamilton's court.

47. Egerton and Paquette, *The Denmark Vesey Affair*, 416.

Chapter Three. With Fear and Trembling

1. Payne, *Recollections of Seventy Years*.

2. No. 2639, An Act to Amend the Law Relating to Slaves and Free Persons of Color. Quoted in Payne, *Recollections of Seventy Years*, 27.

3. Kennedy received his BA in 1807 at the age of twenty and his MA in 1811. Yale University, *Catalogue of the Officers and Graduates*, 28.

4. Egerton and Paquette, *The Denmark Vesey Affair*, 200; emphasis in the original. Kennedy's use of the verb "conjure" may be a play on fact that, as I discuss shortly, Jack was known as a "conjurer" (Hamilton, *An Account*, 36; cf. nn. 8 and 11 in this chapter), although Kennedy uses the same verb when sentencing Vesey. All three of the verdicts Kennedy delivered that were included in the *Official Report* appear in the appendix to this book.

5. The same speech appears in Matthew 3:7–8.

6. Jonathan Edwards's "Sinners in the Hands of an Angry God," 50.

7. Egerton and Paquette, *The Denmark Vesey Affair*, 76.

8. On Jack as a conjurer who utilized traditional African religious practices, consult Rucker, *The River Flows On*, 163–66.

9. Hamilton, *An Account*, 37, 38. Harry had his death sentence reduced to banishment in exchange for his confession.

10. Egerton and Paquette, *The Denmark Vesey Affair*, 199.

11. Hamilton, *An Account*, 35. Yorrick referred to Jack as "a Doctor," although Hamilton glosses the title with the parenthetical qualification "(that is a Conjurer)" (Hamilton, *An Account*, 36). George Vanderhorst testified that Yorrick told him that Jack "had also parched Corn & ground nuts" (Egerton and Paquette, *The Denmark Vesey Affair*, 285).

12. Hamilton, *An Account*, 47.

13. Hamilton, *An Account*, 47.

14. Hamilton, *An Account*, 47.

15. Society of the Cincinnati, *The Original Institution of the General Society of the Cincinnati*, 27.

16. J. Kennedy, *An Oration, Delivered in Saint Philip's Church, before the Inhabitants of Charleston, South-Carolina, on the Fourth of July 1801*.

17. Society of the Cincinnati, *The Original Institution of the General Society of the Cincinnati*, 37.

18. "Cincinnati; South-Carolina; Friday; Lionel H. Kennedy, Esq.; Oration; July; Revolution," *City Gazette and Commercial Daily Advertiser*, February 24, 1813, 3. Lionel Kennedy was not the society's first choice to deliver the oration that year. The article indicates that the invitation came only after William Washington, whose father was George Washington's second cousin and an officer in the Continental Army, declined the offer.

19. L. Kennedy, *An Oration, Delivered in Saint Philip's Church; before the Inhabitants of Charleston, South-Carolina. On Monday the Fifth of July 1813.* As this pamphlet's title indicates, Kennedy delivered his speech on July 5 because July 4 fell on a Sunday in 1813.

20. L. Kennedy, *An Oration*, 3.

21. Joshua 21:13, 27, 32, 38; 1 Chronicles 6:57 (6:42 in Hebrew); cf. Numbers 35:25–28, 32; Deuteronomy 19:2–7.

22. L. Kennedy, *An Oration*, 16. Kennedy's quotation of Fisher Ames comes from *Eulogies and Orations on the Life and Death of General George Washington, First President of the United States of America*, 108. For Kennedy's quotation of John Page, consult Worthington Chauncey Ford, *Some Jefferson Correspondence, 1775–1787*, 17.

23. L. Kennedy, *An Oration*, 21. The quotation comes from Howell and Howell, *A Complete Collection of State Trials and Proceedings*, 1089.

24. Egerton and Paquette, *The Denmark Vesey Affair*, 185. The term "lamp of life" comes from part 6, lines 150–51 in *Queen Mab*, an 1813 poem by Percy Bysshe Shelley. These lines describe the human spirit as something "[t]hat fades not when the lamp of earthly life, Extinguished in the dampness of the grave" (Shelley, *Queen Mab*, 80). The term "from time to eternity" comes from William Penn's collection of sayings first published in 1682: "And this is the comfort of the good, that the grave cannot hold them, and that they live as soon as they die. For death is no more than a turning of us over from time to eternity" (Penn, *Fruits of Solitude*, 99–100).

25. Egerton and Paquette, *The Denmark Vesey Affair*, 263. Kennedy's use of Aesop's fable may have been meant to counter Vesey's appeals to another of Aesop's fables. As noted in the introduction, at Vesey's trial, Joe La Roche testified about Vesey's use of one of Aesop's tales about Hercules and the Waggoner to encourage self-determination among enslaved persons in their struggle for freedom.

26. Egerton and Paquette, *The Denmark Vesey Affair*, 185.

27. Cowper, *Poems*, 188.

28. Egerton and Paquette, *The Denmark Vesey Affair*, 185.

29. Egerton and Paquette, *The Denmark Vesey Affair*, 185.

30. Egerton and Paquette, *The Denmark Vesey Affair*, 263.

31. Scholarship on the uses of Noah's curse in the antebellum era is extensive. For discussions and bibliographies, see Davis, *This Strange Story*; Haynes, *Noah's Curse*;

S. Johnson, *The Myth of Ham in Nineteenth-Century American Christianity*; Peterson, *Ham and Japheth in America*; Schipper, "The Blessing of Ham." On Noah's curse in relation to race, color, and slavery in earlier periods, consult Goldenberg, *The Curse of Ham*; Goldenberg, *Black and Slave*; Reed, "The Injustice of Noah's Curse and the Presumption of Canaanite Guilt"; Schipper, "Religion, Race and the Wife of Ham"; and Whitford, *The Curse of Ham in the Early Modern Era*.

32. Egerton and Paquette, *The Denmark Vesey Affair*, 263.

33. Raymond, *Thoughts on Political Economy*, 18. For examples of proslavery interpretations of Genesis 3:19 in later decades leading up to the Civil War, consult Schipper, "'On Such Texts Comment Is Unnecessary,'" 1044–46.

34. Egerton and Paquette, *The Denmark Vesey Affair*, 185.

35. Egerton and Paquette, *The Denmark Vesey Affair*, 185; emphasis in the original.

36. Egerton and Paquette, *The Denmark Vesey Affair*, 263; emphasis in the original. The short italicized phrase "spirit of truth" also appears in the New Testament. This phrase occurs in John 14:14, 15:26, 16:13; 1 John 4:6.

37. Killens, *Great Gittin' Up Morning*, 125.

Chapter Four. Now Profitable

1. For the full text of this letter, consult Egerton and Paquette, *The Denmark Vesey Affair*, 376–79.

2. Egerton, "'Why They Did Not Preach Up This Thing,'" 311.

3. Palmer, *Religion Profitable*, 14; emphasis in the original.

4. Howe, *History of the Presbyterian Church in South Carolina*, 2:195.

5. Princeton University, *General Catalogue of Princeton University 1746–1906*, 113.

6. These services were separate from the class meetings discussed in the introduction.

7. Moore, "The Abiel Abbot Journals, 70. Quoted in Egerton and Paquette, *The Denmark Vesey Affair*, 31.

8. Consult the discussion in chapter 1.

9. Egerton and Paquette, *The Denmark Vesey Affair*, 377. Beach's description of Rolla's repentance to Palmer, in which he "evinced much feeling & penitence even to tears," is consistent with Rolla's confession to Daniel Hall, in which he allegedly exclaimed, "But if I had read these Psalms, Doctor, which I have read, since I have been in this prison, they would never have got me to join them" (Egerton and Paquette, *The Denmark Vesey Affair*, 167).

10. Egerton and Paquette, *The Denmark Vesey Affair*, 378.

11. Egerton and Paquette, *The Denmark Vesey Affair*, 377.

12. Egerton and Paquette, *The Denmark Vesey Affair*, 378; emphasis in the original.

13. Hamilton, *An Account*, 18.

14. *Liberator* 7.35 (August 23, 1837): 1.

15. Egerton and Paquette, *The Denmark Vesey Affair*, 416; emphasis in the original.

16. Palmer, *Religion Profitable*, 16.

17. Egerton and Paquette, *The Denmark Vesey Affair*, 378.

18. Egerton and Paquette, *The Denmark Vesey Affair*, 159.

19. Palmer, *Religion Profitable*, 11.

20. Palmer, *Religion Profitable*, 6–7.

21. Palmer, *Religion Profitable*, 7.

22. Palmer, *Religion Profitable*, 7.

23. Palmer, *Religion Profitable*, 8.

24. Palmer, *Religion Profitable*, 8.

25. Palmer, *Religion Profitable*, 9.

26. Palmer, *Religion Profitable*, 10.

27. Palmer, *Religion Profitable*, 11.

28. Palmer, *Religion Profitable*, 13; emphasis in the original.

29. Palmer, *Religion Profitable*, 11.

30. Palmer, *Religion Profitable*, 11.

31. Palmer, *Religion Profitable*, 13.

32. Palmer, *Religion Profitable*, 13.

33. For this reason, a slaveholder would not challenge an enslaved person to a duel regardless of how widespread the dueling system may have been in Charleston. On the logic behind the dueling system, consult Greenberg, *Honor and Slavery*. As Stephen R. Haynes convincingly documents, proslavery antebellum intellectuals often interpreted biblical texts from an honor-based prospective (Haynes, *Noah's Curse*, 65–86). The Benjamin M. Palmer whom Haynes discusses in relation to honor and biblical interpretation on pp. 146–60, however, is not the author of *Religion Profitable* but his better-known nephew of the same name.

34. Palmer, *Religion Profitable*, 12.

35. Palmer, *Religion Profitable*, 12.

36. Palmer, *Religion Profitable*, 12; emphasis in the original.

37. Palmer, *Religion Profitable*, 13.

38. The relevant portion of this article reads: "And whereas, many of the slaves in this Province wear clothes much above the condition of slaves, for the procuring whereof they use sinister and evil methods: For the prevention, therefore, of such practices for the future, Be it enacted by the authority aforesaid, That no owner or proprietor of any Negro slave, or other slave, (except livery men and boys,) shall permit or suffer such Negro or other slave, to have or wear any sort of apparel whatsoever, finer, other, or greater value than Negro cloth, duffels, kerseys, osnabrigs, blue

linen, check linen or coarse garlix, or calicoes, checked cottons, or Scotch plaids, under the pain of forfeiting all and every such apparel and garment, that any person shall permit or suffer his Negro or other slave to have or wear, finer, other or of greater value than Negro cloth, duffels, coarse kerseys, osnabrigs, blue linen, check linen or coarse garlix or calicoes, checked cottons or Scotch plaids, as aforesaid; and all and every constable and other persons are hereby authorized, empowered, and re-quired, when as often as they shall find any such Negro slave, or other slave, having or wearing any sort of garment or apparel whatsoever, finer, other or of greater value than Negro cloth, duffels, coarse kerseys, osnabrigs, blue linen, check linen, or coarse garlix, or calicoes, checked cottons or Scottish plaids, as aforesaid, to seize and take away the same, to his or their own use, benefit and behoof; any law, usage or custom to the contrary notwithstanding." For a detailed discussion of "Negro cloth," including its use in the Negro Act of 1740, consult Arabindan-Kesson, *Black Bodies, White Gold*, 42–57.

39. Palmer, *Religion Profitable*, 15.

40. Palmer, *Religion Profitable*, 15; emphasis in the original.

41. Palmer, *Religion Profitable*, 15.

42. Palmer, *Religion Profitable*, 15.

43. Palmer, *Religion Profitable*, 16; emphasis in the original.

44. Palmer, *Religion Profitable*, 21.

45. Palmer, *Religion Profitable*, 18.

46. Palmer, *Religion Profitable*, 19.

47. Palmer, *Religion Profitable*, 19.

Chapter Five. They Shall Be Your Bondmen Forever

1. Egerton and Paquette, *The Denmark Vesey Affair*, 416.

2. Egerton and Paquette, *The Denmark Vesey Affair*, 416; emphasis in the original.

3. Furman, *Exposition of the Views of the Baptists*, 2.

4. Quoted in Paquette and Egerton, "Of Facts and Fables," 41.

5. Quoted in Paquette and Egerton, "Of Facts and Fables," 41.

6. Quoted in Paquette and Egerton, "Of Facts and Fables," 41.

7. Quoted in Paquette and Egerton, "Of Facts and Fables," 40.

8. Paquette and Egerton compared a draft of this letter with fragments from two manuscripts handwritten by Furman. They observe that the letter's nine pages "rep-resent an almost verbatim transcription of two manuscript fragments written by Furman" ("Of Facts and Fables," 14).

9. Quoted in Paquette and Egerton, "Of Facts and Fables," 40.

10. The fact that the letter paraphrases Colossians 4:1, another text that Palmer discusses in his sermon, makes his influence on the letter even more likely. For a discussion of this verse, consult chapter 4.

11. Quoted in Paquette and Egerton, "Of Facts and Fables," 40.

12. Quoted in Paquette and Egerton, "Of Facts and Fables," 40.

13. Hamilton, *An Account*, 2.

14. Egerton and Paquette, *The Denmark Vesey Affair*, 416.

15. Quoted in Paquette and Egerton, "Of Facts and Fables," 44.

16. Cited in Ludlum, *Early American Hurricanes*, 115.

17. Simms, *The History of South Carolina*, 328.

18. Buist, "On the Doctrine of Particular Providence."

19. Buist, "On the Doctrine of Particular Providence," 120. Buist does not focus on the storm or Vesey's intended insurrection, which he only mentions near the end of his sermon. Instead, his focus is the nature of providence, arguing that God continues to guide and intervene in natural and human affairs rather than simply leaving humans and the rest of nature to their own devices after God created them, a doctrine that he refers to as "general providence."

20. Buist, "On the Doctrine of Particular Providence," 120.

21. Buist, "On the Doctrine of Particular Providence," 121.

22. Furman, *Exposition of the Views of the Baptists*, 3

23. Furman, *Exposition of the Views of the Baptists*, 9.

24. Furman, *Exposition of the Views of the Baptists*, 9.

25. Furman, *Exposition of the Views of the Baptists*, 7.

26. Furman, *Exposition of the Views of the Baptists*, 7.

27. Furman, *Exposition of the Views of the Baptists*, 4. It is possible that Furman is referring to the former governor, Thomas Bennett Jr. here.

28. Furman, *Exposition of the Views of the Baptists*, 7. Similarly, the letter by the society's board of managers to Governor Bennett acknowledges that the idea that the Bible is against slavery is "a sentiment which many, & some very worthy Men have advanced." Quoted in Paquette and Egerton, "Of Facts and Fables," 40.

29. Furman, *Exposition of the Views of the Baptists*, 13.

30. Egerton and Paquette, *The Denmark Vesey Affair*, 78. Similarly, as mentioned in the introduction, Hamilton notes that, as a young man, Vesey was recognized for his "beauty, alertness and intelligence" (Hamilton, *An Account*, 16).

31. To be clear, Vesey and the biblical texts that he allegedly used are noted, although not rebutted, in the published trial transcripts and various newspaper articles, but not in the sermons or theological works by prominent white clergy in Charleston in the wake of the trials and executions.

32. Furman, *Exposition of the Views of the Baptists*, 7.

33. Furman, *Exposition of the Views of the Baptists*, 7.

34. Saffin, "A Brief and Candid Answer," 253. Saffin responds to Sewall's use of Exodus 21:16 by noting that just a few verses earlier, in Exodus 21:1–11, there are guidelines for how Israelites should treat those whom they enslave. He writes, "in that very chapter [that Sewall cites] there is a dispensation to the people of Israel,

to have bond men, women and children, even of their own nation in some cases [Exodus 21:2]; and rules given therein to be observed concerning them; Verse the 4th [Exodus 21:4]" (253).

35. Edwards, *The Injustice and Impolicy of the Slave Trade*, 15.

36. Edwards, *The Injustice and Impolicy of the Slave Trade*, 18.

37. Edwards, *The Injustice and Impolicy of the Slave Trade*, 19.

38. Gleig and Macfarquhar, *Encyclopædia Britannica*, 17:522–32.

39. Gleig and Macfarquhar, *Encyclopædia Britannica*, 17:523. In the margin of this page, Gleig and Macfarquhar mistakenly refer to Exodus 21:16 as Leviticus 21:16.

40. The Fugitive Slave Clause reads, "No person held to service or labour in one state, under the laws thereof, escaping into another, shall, in consequence of any law or regulation therein, be discharged from such service or labour, but shall be delivered up on claim of the party to whom such service or labour may be due." The language is similar to article 6 of the Northwest Ordinance for the Government of the Territory of the United States, North-West of the River Ohio, popularly known as the Northwest Ordinance, an act passed in 1787 by the Congress of the Confederation. In part, article 6 reads, "any person escaping into the same [the northwest territory], from whom labor or service is lawfully claimed in any one of the original States, such fugitive may be lawfully reclaimed, and conveyed to the person claiming his or her labor or service as aforesaid." On the use of biblical texts in nineteenth century debates over the fugitive slave clause, consult Couey and Schipper, "Hide the Outcasts."

41. Benton, *Abridgment of the Debates of Congress, from 1789 to 1856*, 6:35.

42. Benton, *Abridgment of the Debates of Congress*, 6:38.

43. Benton, *Abridgment of the Debates of Congress*, 6:39.

44. Benton, *Abridgment of the Debates of Congress*, 6:39.

45. Holland, *Refutation of the Calumnies*, 41–42.

46. For examples of these criticisms, consult chapter 2.

47. Holland, *Refutation of the Calumnies*, 77.

48. Holland, *Refutation of the Calumnies*, 12.

49. Furman, *Exposition of the Views of the Baptists*, 8.

50. Furman, *Exposition of the Views of the Baptists*, 12.

51. Furman, *Exposition of the Views of the Baptists*, 10. Although the rampant rape of enslaved women by their slaveholders is well documented, Furman's claim that a slaveholder can be a "father of his slaves" probably refers to a male slaveholder's paternalistic rather than biological relationship to those whom he enslaves.

52. Furman, *Exposition of the Views of the Baptists*, 10.

53. Freehling, "Denmark Vesey's Antipaternalistic Reality," 35.

54. Furman, *Exposition of the Views of the Baptists*, 10.

55. Furman, *Exposition of the Views of the Baptists*, 11.

56. Furman, *Exposition of the Views of the Baptists*, 10–11.

57. Egerton and Paquette, *The Denmark Vesey Affair*, 665.

58. For a classic discussion of the "necessary evil" idea of slavery, consult Freehling, *Prelude to Civil War*, 76–82.

59. Holland, *Refutation of the Calumnies*, 22.

60. Furman, *Exposition of the Views of the Baptists*, 13.

61. Egerton and Paquette, *The Denmark Vesey Affair*, 263; emphasis in the original. Consult the appendix for the full text of Kennedy's sentence of the ten enslaved persons.

62. Egerton and Paquette, *The Denmark Vesey Affair*, 263.

63. Egerton and Paquette, *The Denmark Vesey Affair*, 263.

64. Herbemont, *Observations Suggested by the Late Occurrences in Charleston*, 6–7. To be clear, Herbemont was conflicted over this horrific conclusion, noting, "But God forbid that such a plan be adopted! Humanity forbids it, and when we have recourse to severe punishments, it ought to be only in obedience to the commands of the most imperious necessity" (7).

65. Hamilton, *An Account*, 2. On Hamilton's account as a response to charges of leniency, consult Freehling, "Denmark Vesey's Antipaternalistic Reality," 3).

66. Furman, *Exposition of the Views of the Baptists*, 18.

Chapter Six. For He Is His Money

1. Quoted in January, "The South Carolina Association," 193.

2. For a list of members of the South Carolina Association, consult Egerton and Paquette, *The Denmark Vesey Affair*, 611–19.

3. Ford, *Deliver Us from Evil*, 279.

4. On the South Carolina Association's enforcement and defense of the Negro Seaman Act, consult Ford, *Deliver Us from Evil*, 282–91.

5. Dalcho, *Practical Considerations Founded on the Scriptures*, 3–4; emphasis in the original. Dalcho combines 1 Timothy 2:4 and Ephesians 4:21 in this quotation. The phrase "as it is in Jesus" does not appear in 1 Timothy 2:4 but comes from Ephesians 4:21. In the King James Version, 1 Timothy 2:4 ends with "the knowledge of the truth." Ephesians 4:21 reads, "If so be that ye have heard him, and have been taught by him, as the truth *is in Jesus*" (emphasis added).

6. Furman, *Exposition of the Views of the Baptists*, 7, 18. For representative examples of scholarship that compares Dalcho and Furman's pamphlets, consult Egerton, *He Shall Go Out Free*, 219–21; Ford, *Deliver Us from Evil*, 253–67; Young, *Domesticating Slavery*, 168–71.

7. Dalcho, *Practical Considerations Founded on the Scriptures*, 22.

8. Dalcho, *Practical Considerations Founded on the Scriptures*, 8. Dalcho writes, "It was not my original intention to have gone into a minute detail of the origin of slavery;

but as I think the *Exposition* published by the Baptists, places it on insufficient ground, I shall briefly state what appears to me to be scriptural authority on the subject" (8–9).

9. Dalcho, *Practical Considerations Founded on the Scriptures*, 4.

10. Dalcho, *Practical Considerations Founded on the Scriptures*, 5.

11. On Dow's trial and conviction in Charleston, consult Dow, *The Stranger in Charleston!*.

12. Egerton and Paquette, *The Denmark Vesey Affair*, 323. This testimony is not included in the *Official Report* but appears in "Evidence Document B." Perault is Perault Strohecker, who was enslaved by a blacksmith named John Strohecker.

13. Dalcho, *Practical Considerations Founded on the Scriptures*, 5; emphasis in the original.

14. On slavery as a "necessary evil," consult the discussion in chapter 5.

15. Dalcho, *Practical Considerations Founded on the Scriptures*, 6.

16. Dalcho, *Practical Considerations Founded on the Scriptures*, 6. Founded in 1816, the American Colonization Society supported the migration to Africa of free and formerly enslaved persons of African descent living in the United States. Beginning in 1821, the society helped to establish Liberia in western Africa as a colony for this project.

17. Dalcho, *Practical Considerations Founded on the Scriptures*, 6.

18. In response to critics in non-slaveholding states, Dalcho may also imply that this point about southerners voluntarily giving up their land could apply to the non-slaveholding states as well, if their citizens returned their lands to Native Americans.

19. Dalcho, *Practical Considerations Founded on the Scriptures*, 8.

20. Dalcho, *Practical Considerations Founded on the Scriptures*, 10.

21. Dalcho, *Practical Considerations Founded on the Scriptures*, 19.

22. Dalcho, *Practical Considerations Founded on the Scriptures*, 11.

23. For a detailed discussion of Dalcho's interpretation of the descendants of Canaan, consult Schipper "'Misconstruction of the Sacred Page.'"

24. Dalcho charged that the descendants of Ham had a pattern of usurpation. He claimed that the descendants of Ham's son Cush usurped the land of Shinar (which he spells "Shinaar") from Asshur, who, like Abram, was a descendant of Shem (Genesis 10:22). He arrived at this conclusion because, according to Genesis 10:10–11, Nimrod, the grandson of Ham, establishes his kingdom "in the land of Shinar" and "[o]ut of that land went forth Asshur." Dalcho understands the latter phrase to mean that Nimrod forced Asshur into exile from the land of Shinar. This interpretation of Nimrod as an illegitimate usurper has a long history that began well before Dalcho's birth. Algernon Sidney's *Discourses concerning Government*, published posthumously in 1698, is a lengthy treatise that challenges the divine right of monarchy. Sidney, a

British political philosopher, believed that individuals should be able to choose their own form of government. In the opening chapter of *Discourses*, Sidney traces the tyranny of kingship back to Nimrod. He writes, "As to earthly Kings, the first of 'em was *Nimrod*, the sixth Son of *Chush* the Son of *Ham*, *Noah's* younger and accursed Son" (Sidney, *Discourses concerning Government*, 16; emphasis in the original). Indeed, the first mention of kings or kingdoms in the Bible occurs in Genesis 10:10: "And the beginning of his [Nimrod's] kingdom was Babel, and Erech, and Accad, and Calneh, in the land of Shinar." The Bible does not elaborate on the nature of Nimrod's reign because his entire story is covered in only five verses buried deep within a biblical genealogy (Genesis 10:8–12; cf. 1 Chronicles 1:10). Nevertheless, Sidney had strong opinions about Nimrod's reign. "This Kingdom of *Nimrod* was an Usurpation, void of all Right, proceeding from the most violent and mischievous Vices," Sidney exclaimed. "[T]he best Interpreters call [Nimrod] a cruel Tyrant" (16). This leads him to conclude, "Whosoever therefore like *Nimrod* grounds his pretensions of Right upon Usurpation and Tyranny, declares himself to be, like *Nimrod*, a Usurper and a Tyrant, that is, an Enemy to God and Man, and to have no Right at all" (20). Sidney also argues that Nimrod was a usurper who acquired his kingdom through conquest because he would not have inherited a kingdom from his father because of his low position in the birth order of his siblings (16–17). Genesis 10:7–8 lists Nimrod last among the six sons of Cush: "And the sons of Cush; Seba, and Havilah, and Sabtah, and Raamah, and Sabtechah . . . And Cush begat Nimrod: he began to be a mighty one in the earth." By the end of the eighteenth century, the idea that Nimrod was a tyrannical king and a usurper was so well established that it was recorded in the entry on "slavery" in the 1797 edition of the *Encyclopædia Britannica*:

> [T]here can be little doubt but that he [Nimrod] became a mighty one by violence; for being the sixth son of his father, and apparently much younger than the other five, it is not likely that his inheritance exceeded theirs either in extent or in population. He enlarged it, however, by conquest; for it appears from Scripture, that he invaded the territories of Assur the son of Shem, who had settled in Shinar; and obliging him to remove into Assyria, he seized upon Babylon, and made it the capital of the first kingdom in the world. (Gleig and Macfarquhar, *Encyclopædia Britannica*, 17:523)

According to the argument in *Encyclopædia Britannica*, Nimrod must have seized power illegitimately through violence and conquest because, being a lowly sixth in line for the throne, he would not have inherited his kingdom. More recently, in contrast to those who characterize Nimrod as a tyrant, Anthony Pinn has argued that African American humanists can reclaim Nimrod as a champion of human ingenuity and consider themselves to be "children of Nimrod." Consult Anthony B. Pinn, *African American Humanistic Principles*; and Pinn and Callahan, *African American Religious Life and the Story of Nimrod*.

25. Dalcho, *Practical Considerations Founded on the Scriptures*, 12–13; emphasis in the original.

26. Dalcho, *Practical Considerations Founded on the Scriptures*, 13; emphasis in the original.

27. Dalcho, *Practical Considerations Founded on the Scriptures*, 13.

28. Dalcho, *Practical Considerations Founded on the Scriptures*, 18.

29. Dalcho, *Practical Considerations Founded on the Scriptures*, 20–25. Several months earlier, Benjamin Palmer had offered detailed interpretations of these New Testament texts in his influential sermon *Religion Profitable*, discussed in chapter 4. Dalcho does not examine these texts in nearly the same level of detail as Palmer. Instead, he often quotes one and quickly moves on to another.

30. Dalcho, *Practical Considerations Founded on the Scriptures*, 25.

31. Dalcho, *Practical Considerations Founded on the Scriptures*, 33.

32. Dalcho, *Practical Considerations Founded on the Scriptures*, 32.

33. By contrast, well before Dalcho wrote his pamphlet, antislavery interpreters cited sources from late antiquity to argue the some of the Canaanites fled north to Phoenicia (near modern-day Lebanon) rather than south to Africa. According to this argument, these Canaanites became the ancestors of white English slaveholders rather than enslaved Africans. For an example, in 1787, Cugoano referred to the Canaanites who Joshua chased out of the land as the people "who settled in the northwest of Canaan, and formed the once flourishing states of Tyre and Sidon." According to Joshua 11:8, Joshua and the Israelites defeated a coalition of Canaanite rulers "and chased them unto great Zidon." Zidon, also spelled Sidon, was a prosperous Phoenician seaport city near Tyre north of Canaan (Genesis 10:19, 49:13; Zechariah 9:2). Sidon is also the name of Canaan's oldest son and one of Ham's grandsons (Genesis 10:15). Focusing on those who fled north, Cugoano continues, "Many of the Canaanites who fled away in the Time of Joshua, became mingled with the different nations, and some historians think that some of them came to England. . . . [T]here may be some of the descendants of that wicked generation still subsisting among the [English] slave-holders in the West-Indies" (*Thoughts and Sentiments*, 35, 36). Here Cugoano refers to the theory held by some seventeenth- and eighteenth-century British historians that the Phoenicians had discovered islands, possibly the Isles of Scilly, off the coast of England. The theory elaborates on a vague claim made by Strabo, a first-century BCE geographer, in his *Geographia* (3.5.11). In his notes to Cugoano's narrative, Vincent Carretta, the editor of the 1999 Penguin edition, lists some early British historians who made this claim (*Thoughts and Sentiments*, 158n48).

34. Dalcho, *Practical Considerations Founded on the Scriptures*, 26.

35. Dalcho, *Practical Considerations Founded on the Scriptures*, 31.

36. Dalcho, *Practical Considerations Founded on the Scriptures*, 33, 34; emphasis in the original. On class leadership in the African Church, consult the introduction.

37. Furman, *Exposition of the Views of the Baptists*, 16–17; parenthetical material in the original.

38. Dalcho, *Practical Considerations Founded on the Scriptures*, 36; emphasis in the original.

39. Andrew, "Letters on Methodist History: Letter II," 25.

40. Dalcho, *Practical Considerations Founded on the Scriptures*, 34–35.

41. Dalcho, *Practical Considerations Founded on the Scriptures*, 31.

42. Dalcho, *Practical Considerations Founded on the Scriptures*, 32; emphasis in the original. Note that, with the exception of the stories of Joshua and David's military campaigns, the biblical texts that Vesey allegedly used to justify an insurrection came mostly from the Pentateuch, the first five book of the Bible, and from prophetic books such as Isaiah or Zechariah. By contrast, Dalcho and other proslavery clergy appealed to Psalms, Proverbs, and especially New Testament texts. For example, according to Rolla's confession, Dr. Daniel Hall was said to have shown him some unspecified psalms while Rolla was in jail. Also, Kennedy quoted from Proverbs and, like Palmer and Dalcho, made heavy use of New Testament texts when he sentenced Vesey and his associates to death. In other words, the "practical lessons" in these tracts would come from the parts of the Bible often used to support slavery while skipping over the parts used to support revolt. While ostensibly offering proper religious instruction from the Bible, the tracts that Dalcho suggests would limit people of African descent's access to the contents of the Bible.

Epilogue. No Respecter of Persons

1. "A Colored American" [pseudonym], *The Late Contemplated Insurrection in Charleston*, 8.

2. Neilson, *Recollections of a Six Years' Residence in the United States of America*, 296.

3. Egerton and Paquette, *The Denmark Vesey Affair*, 418.

4. "A Colored American," *The Late Contemplated Insurrection in Charleston*, 8.

5. "A Colored American," *The Late Contemplated Insurrection in Charleston*, 8.

6. For example, Acts 10:34 was associated with Robert Purvis, a mixed race native of Charleston who settled in Philadelphia and became one of the nation's leading abolitionists. At his memorial held at Bethel African Methodist Episcopal Church in Philadelphia on April 18, 1898, a resolution was read that ended with the line "he passed into the presence of 'Him who is' no respecter of persons" (quoted in Beacon, *But One Race*, 210). Since Purvis, who was living in Charleston when William Dove was elected as captain of the City Guard, referred to himself in his writings as a "colored American," Egerton and Paquette tentatively suggest that Purvis may have been the author of *The Late Contemplated Insurrection in Charleston* (Egerton and Paquette, *The Denmark Vesey Affair*, 738–39).

7. "A Colored American," *The Late Contemplated Insurrection in Charleston*, 8.

8. On the campaign to build the Denmark Vesey monument and the opposition to it, consult Dykens, "Commemoration and Controversy," 103–28; and Kytle and Roberts, *Denmark Vesey's Garden*, 330–36. At some point during the weekend of May 29–30, 2021, vandals severely damaged the monument. They created a deep crack that cuts across the name "Demark Vesey" that is inscribed in large letters near the top of the pedestal. The name appears to have been the focus of the vandalism. That the monument was defaced over the 2021 Memorial Day weekend is probably not a coincidence. During the Civil War, the site that later became Hampton Park was a racecourse that served as an outdoor prison for Union soldiers. Over 250 of these soldiers died and were buried in a mass grave at this site. As the war ended, African Americans led the effort to build a new cemetery and reinter the fallen soldiers. On May 1, 1865, they held a ceremony, now recognized as the first Memorial Day celebration, that included a parade led by nearly three thousand Black schoolchildren. A marker with the title "First Memorial Day in the United States of America" was set up in Hampton Park in 2010 to commemorate these events publicly. For a brief account of this first Memorial Day, consult Blight, "Forgetting Why We Remember."

9. Reverend Pinckney's entire sermon is available on YouTube, http://www.youtube.com/watch?v=l6T6OxSVkrU; cf. Blight, "Clementa Pinckney, a Martyr of Reconciliation."

10. "A Colored American," *The Late Contemplated Insurrection in Charleston*, 5.

11. Consult the preface to this book.

Appendix

1. Hamilton, *An Account*, 16–17.

2. Egerton and Paquette, *The Denmark Vesey Affair*, 184–85; emphasis in the original.

3. Egerton and Paquette, *The Denmark Vesey Affair*, 200; emphasis in the original. Cf. Hamilton, *An Account*, 47.

4. Egerton and Paquette, *The Denmark Vesey Affair*, 262–63, 265; emphasis in the original. Cf. Hamilton, *An Account*, 47–48.

BIBLIOGRAPHY

Acts and Resolutions of the General Assembly of the State of South-Carolina, Passed in December, 1805. Columbia: D. and J. J. Faust, State Printers, 1806.

Andrew, James Osgood. "Letters on Methodist History: Letter II." *Methodist Magazine and Quarterly Review* 12 (January 1830): 22–25.

Arabindan-Kesson, Anne. *Black Bodies, White Gold: Art, Cotton, and Commerce in the Atlantic World.* Durham, NC: Duke University Press, 2021.

Bailey, N. Louise. *Biographical Directory of the South Carolina House of Representatives,* vol. 4, 1791–1815. 5 vols. Columbia. University of South Carolina Press, 1984.

Bassard, Katherine Clay. *Transforming Scriptures: African American Women Writers and the Bible.* Athens: University of Georgia Press, 2010.

Beacon, Margaret Hope. *But One Race: The Life of Robert Purvis.* Albany: State University of New York Press, 2007.

Benton, Thomas Hart. *Abridgment of the Debates of Congress, from 1789 to 1856.* 16 vols. New York: D. Appleton and Co., 1858.

Bibb, Henry. *Slave Insurrection in 1831, in Southampton County, VA., Headed by Nat Turner, also a Conspiracy of Slaves, in Charleston, South Carolina, in 1822.* New York: Henry Bibb, 1849.

Blight, David W. "Clementa Pinckney, a Martyr of Reconciliation." *Atlantic,* June 22, 2015, https://www.theatlantic.com/politics/archive/2015/06/pinckney-charleston-civil-war-150-years/396455.

———. "Forgetting Why We Remember." *New York Times,* May 30, 2011, A19.

Booth, Abraham. *Commerce in the Human Species, and the Enslaving of Innocent Persons, Inimical to the Laws of Moses and the Gospel of Christ: A Sermon, Preached in Little Prescot Street, Goodman's Fields, January 29, 1792.* London: L. Wayland, 1792.

Bourne, George. *The Book and Slavery Irreconcilable with Animadversions upon Dr. Smith's Philosophy.* Philadelphia: J. M. Sanderson and Co., 1816.

Bradford, William and George H. Moore. "The First Printed Protest against Slavery in America." *The Pennsylvania Magazine of History and Biography* 13.3 (Oct., 1889): 265–70.

Brawley, Benjamin Griffith. *A Short History of the American Negro*. New York: Macmillan Company, 1913.

Brown, William Wells. *The Black Man: His Antecedents, His Genius, and His Achievements*. Boston: R. F. Wallcut, 1863.

Buist, Arthur. "On the Doctrine of Particular Providence." In *The Southern Preacher: A Collection of Sermons, from the Manuscripts of Several Eminent Ministers of the Gospel Residing in the Southern States. Carefully Selected from the Original Manuscripts, with the Consent and Approbation of Their Respective Authors. Together with a Few Post-Humous Sermons, from the Manuscripts of Eminent Deceased Ministers, Who, When Living, Had Resided in the Southern States. Carefully Selected from the Original Manuscripts, with the Consent and Approbation of Those in Whose Possession They Were Found*, edited by Colin McIver, 107–24. Philadelphia: William Fry, 1824.

Callahan, Allen Dwight. *The Talking Bible: African Americans and the Bible*. New Haven, CT: Yale University Press, 2006.

"Cincinnati; South-Carolina; Friday; Lionel H. Kennedy, Esq.; Oration; July; Revolution." *City Gazette and Commercial Daily Advertiser*, February 24, 1813, 3.

Coffey, John. *Exodus and Liberation: Deliverance Politics from John Calvin to Martin Luther King Jr*. New York: Oxford University Press, 2014.

"A Colored American" [pseudonym]. *The Late Contemplated Insurrection in Charleston, S.C. with the Execution of Thirty-Six of the Patriots: The Death of William Irving, the Provoked Husband, and Joe Devaul, for Refusing to Be the Slave of Mr. Roach: With the Capture of the American Slaver Trading between the Seat of Government and New Orleans: Together with an Account of the Capture of the Spanish Schooner Amistad*. New York: Printed for the Publisher, 1850.

Couey, J. Blake, and Jeremy Schipper, "Hide the Outcasts: Isaiah 16:3–4 and Fugitive Slave Laws." *Harvard Theological Review* (forthcoming).

Cowper, William. *Poems*. London: J. Johnson, 1782.

Crèvecoeur, J. Hector St. John de. *Letters from an American Farmer; Describing Certain Provincial Situations, Manners, and Customs Not Generally Known; and Conveying Some Idea of the Late and Present Interior Circumstances of the British Colonies in North America*. London: Thomas Davies, 1782.

Cross, Wilbur. *Gullah Culture in America*. Westport, CT: Praeger, 2008.

Cugoano, Ottobah. *Thoughts and Sentiments on the Evil and Wicked Traffic of the Slavery and Commerce of the Human Species: Humbly Submitted to the Inhabitants of Great-Britain*. London: N.p., 1787.

———. *Thoughts and Sentiments on the Evil of Slavery and Other Writings*. Edited by Vincent Carretta. New York: Penguin Books, 1999.

Dalcho, Frederick. *Practical Considerations Founded on the Scriptures, Relative to the Slave Population of South-Carolina*. Charleston, SC: A. E. Miller, 1823.

Davis, Stacy. *This Strange Story: Jewish and Christian Interpretation of the Curse of Canaan from Antiquity to 1865.* Latham, MD: University Press of America, 2008.

Dow, Lorenzo. *The Stranger in Charleston! Or, The Trial and Confession of Lorenzo Dow, Addressed to the United States in General. and South-Carolina in Particular.* 2nd ed. Philadelphia: Reprinted for the Purchaser, 1822.

DuBois, W.E.B., ed. *The Negro Church: A Social Study Made under the Direction of Atlanta University by the Eighth Atlanta Conference.* Atlanta: Atlanta University Press, 1903.

Dykens, Sarah Katherine. "Commemoration and Controversy: The Memorialization of Denmark Vesey in Charleston, South Carolina." Master's thesis, Clemson University, 2015.

Edwards, Jonathan (the elder). *Jonathan Edwards's "Sinners in the Hands of an Angry God": A Casebook.* Edited by Wilson H. Kimnach, Caleb J. D. Maskell, and Kenneth P. Minkema. New Haven, CT: Yale University Press, 2010.

Edwards, Jonathan (the younger). *The Injustice and Impolicy of the Slave Trade, and of the Slavery of the Africans: Illustrated in a Sermon Preached before the Connecticut Society for the Promotion of Freedom, and for the Relief of Persons Unlawfully Holden in Bondage, at Their Annual Meeting in New-Haven, Sept. 15, 1791* Boston: Wells and Lilly, 1822.

Egerton, Douglas R. *He Shall Go Out Free: The Lives of Denmark Vesey.* Rev. and updated ed. Lanham, MD: Rowman and Littlefield, 2004.

———. "'Why They Did Not Preach Up This Thing': Denmark Vesey and Revolutionary Theology." *South Carolina Historical Magazine* 100, no. 4 (October 1999): 298–318.

Egerton, Douglas R., and Robert L. Paquette, eds. *The Denmark Vesey Affair: A Documentary History.* Gainesville: University of Florida Press, 2017.

Eulogies and Orations on the Life and Death of General George Washington, First President of the United States of America. No editor identified, Boston: Manning and Loring, 1800.

"Extract from 'Letters from an American Farmer' by J. Hector St. John, a Farmer in Pennsylvania." *American Museum, or Repository of Ancient and Modern Fugitive Pieces &c* 1, no. 3 (March 1787): 209–11.

Ford, Lacy K., Jr. *Deliver Us from Evil: The Slavery Question in the Old South.* New York: Oxford University Press, 2009.

———. "An Interpretation of the Denmark Vesey Insurrection Scare." In *The Proceedings of the South Carolina Historical Association,* edited by Robert Figueira and Stephen Lowe, 7–22. Charleston: South Carolina Historical Association, 2012.

Ford, Worthington Chauncey. *Some Jefferson Correspondence, 1775–1787.* Boston: Press of D. Clapp and Son, 1902.

Fox-Genovese, Elizabeth, and Eugene D. Genovese. *The Mind of the Master Class: History and Faith in the Southern Slaveholders' Worldview.* New York: Cambridge University Press, 2005.

Freehling, William W. "Denmark Vesey's Antipaternalistic Reality." In *The Reintegration of American History: Slavery and the Civil War*, edited by William W. Freehling, 34–58. New York: Oxford University Press, 1994.

———. *Prelude to Civil War: The Nullification Controversy of South Carolina 1816–1836*. New York: Oxford University Press, 1965.

Furman, Richard. *Rev. Dr. Richard Furman's Exposition of the Views of the Baptists, Relative to the Coloured Population of the United States, in a Communication to the Governor of South-Carolina*. Charleston, SC: A. E. Miller, 1823.

Genovese, Eugene D. *Roll, Jordan, Roll: The World the Slaves Made*. New York: Pantheon, 1974.

Glaude, Eddie S., Jr. *Exodus! Religion, Race, and Nation in Early Nineteenth-Century Black America*. Chicago: University of Chicago Press, 2000.

Gleig, George, and Colin Macfarquhar, eds. *Encyclopædia Britannica; or, A Dictionary of Arts, Sciences, and Miscellaneous Literature*. 18 vols. 3rd ed. Edinburgh: A. Bell and C. Macfarquhar, 1797.

Goldenberg, David M. *Black and Slave: The Origins and History of the Curse of Ham*. Studies in the Bible and Its Reception, 10. Berlin: De Gruyter, 2017.

———. *The Curse of Ham: Race and Slavery in Early Judaism, Christianity, and Islam*. Princeton, NJ: Princeton University Press, 2003.

Greenberg, Kenneth S. *Honor and Slavery: Lies, Duels, Noses, Masks, Dressing as a Woman, Gifts, Strangers, Humanitarianism, Death, Slave Rebellions, the Proslavery Argument, Baseball, Hunting, and Gambling in the Old South*. Princeton, NJ: Princeton University Press, 1996.

Grimké, Archibald Henry. *Right on the Scaffold: or, The Martyrs of 1822*. Washington, DC: Academy, 1901.

Gross, Robert A., ed. "Forum: The Making of a Slave Conspiracy, Part 2." *William and Mary Quarterly* 59 (2002): 135–202.

Hamilton, James, Jr., ed. *An Account of the Late Intended Insurrection among a Portion of the Blacks of This City*. Charleston, SC: Corporation of Charleston, 1822.

Haynes, Stephen R. *Noah's Curse: The Biblical Justification of American Slavery*. New York: Oxford University Press, 2002.

Henry, Howell Meadoes. "The Police Control of the Slave in South Carolina." PhD diss., Vanderbilt University, 1914.

Herbemont, Nicholas. *Observations Suggested by the Late Occurrences in Charleston*. Columbia, SC: State Gazette Office, 1822.

Higginson, Thomas Wentworth. "Denmark Vesey." *Atlantic Monthly* 7 (June 1861): 728–44.

Hill Edwards, Justene. *Unfree Markets: The Slaves' Economy and the Rise of Capitalism in South Carolina*. New York: Columbia University Press, 2021.

Hinks, Peter P. *To Awaken My Afflicted Brethren: David Walker and the Problem of Antebellum Slave Resistance*. University Park: Pennsylvania State University Press, 1997.

Hoffer, Peter Charles. *Cry Liberty: The Great Stono River Slave Rebellion of 1739*. New York: Oxford University Press, 2010.

Holland, Edwin C. *Refutation of the Calumnies Circulated against the Southern & Western States Respecting the Institution and Existence of Slavery among Them*. Charleston, SC: A. E. Miller, 1822.

Howe, George. *History of the Presbyterian Church in South Carolina*. 2 vols. Charleston, SC: W. J. Duffie, 1883.

Howell, Thomas Bayly, and Thomas Jones Howell. *A Complete Collection of State Trials and Proceedings for High Treason and Other Crimes and Misdemeanors from the Earliest Period to the Year 1783 with Notes and Other Illustrations and Continued from 1783 to the Present Time*, vol. 22. London: T. C. Hansard, 1817.

January, Alan F. "The South Carolina Association: An Agency for Race Control in Antebellum Charleston." *South Carolina Historical Magazine* 78, no. 3 (1977): 191–201.

Johnson, Michael P. "Denmark Vesey and His Co-conspirators." *William and Mary Quarterly* 58 (2001): 915–76.

Johnson, Sylvester. *The Myth of Ham in Nineteenth-Century American Christianity: Race, Heathens, and the People of God*. New York: Palgrave Macmillan, 2004.

Junior, Nyasha, and Jeremy Schipper. *Black Samson: The Untold Story of an American Icon*. New York: Oxford University Press, 2020.

Kennedy, James. *An Oration, Delivered in Saint Philip's Church, before the Inhabitants of Charleston, South-Carolina, on the Fourth of July 1801; In Commemoration of American Independence by Captain James Kennedy of the South-Carolina Society of Cincinnati, Published at the Request of That Society, and also of the American Revolution Society*. Charleston, SC: W. P. Young, 1801.

Kennedy, Lionel Henry. *An Oration, Delivered in Saint Philip's Church; before the Inhabitants of Charleston, South-Carolina. On Monday the Fifth of July 1813, (the Fourth Being Sunday,) in Commemoration of American Independence; by Appointment of the South-Carolina Society of Cincinnati, and Published at the Request of That Society, and also, of the American Revolution Society*. Charleston, SC: W. P. Young, 1813.

Kennedy, Lionel Henry, and Thomas Parker, eds. *An Official Report of the Trial of the Sundry Negroes Charged with an Attempt to Raise an Insurrection in the State of South Carolina Preceded by an Introduction and a Narrative; and in an Appendix, a Report of the Trials of the Four White Persons on Indictment for Attempting to Excite the Slaves to Insurrection*. Charleston, SC: James R. Schenk, 1822.

Killens, John Oliver. *Great Gittin' Up Morning: A Biography of Denmark Vesey*. New York: Doubleday, 1972.

———, ed. *The Trial Record of Denmark Vesey*. Boston: Beacon, 1970.

Kytle, Ethan J., and Blain Roberts. *Denmark Vesey's Garden: Slavery and Memory in the Cradle of the Confederacy.* New York: New Press, 2018.

The Liberator 7, no. 35 (August 23, 1837): 1. No title provided.

Lofton, John. *Insurrection in South Carolina: The Turbulent World of Denmark Vesey.* Yellow Springs, OH: Antioch Press, 1964.

Ludlum, David M. *Early American Hurricanes, 1492–1870.* Boston: American Meteorological Society, 1963.

Marbury, Herbert Robinson. *Pillars of Cloud and Fire: The Politics of African American Biblical Interpretation.* New York: New York University Press, 2015.

McCarter, P. Kyle, Jr. *1 Samuel: A New Translation with Introduction and Commentary.* Anchor Bible Series, vol. 8. New York: Doubleday, 1980.

Moore, John Hammond, ed. "The Abiel Abbot Journals: A Yankee Preacher in Charleston Society, 1818–1827." *South Carolina Historical Magazine* 68, no. 2 (1967): 51–73.

Neilson, Peter. *Recollections of a Six Years' Residence in the United States of America, Interspersed with Original Anecdotes.* Glasgow: D. Robertson, 1830.

Noll, Mark. *The Civil War as a Theological Crisis.* Chapel Hill: University of North Carolina Press, 2006.

Old South Leaflets. No editor identified. Boston: Directors of the Old South Work, 1900.

Oshatz, Molly. *Slavery and Sin: The Fight against Slavery and the Rise of Liberal Protestantism.* New York: Oxford University Press, 2011.

Palmer, Benjamin Morgan. *Religion Profitable: With a Special Reference to the Case of Servants; A Sermon Preached on September 22, 1822, in the Circular Church, Charleston, S.C.* Charleston, SC: J. R. Schenck, 1822.

Paquette, Robert L. "From Rebellion to Revisionism: The Continuing Debate about the Denmark Vesey Affair." *Journal of the Historical Society* 4 (2004): 314–17.

Paquette, Robert L., and Douglas R. Egerton. "Of Facts and Fables: New Light on the Denmark Vesey Affair." *South Carolina Historical Magazine* 105, no. 1 (January 2004): 8–48.

Payne, Daniel Alexander. *Recollections of Seventy Years: With an Introduction by F. J. Grimke; Compiled and Arranged by Sarah C. Bierce Scarborough.* Edited by C. S. Smith. Nashville, TN: Publishing House of the A.M.E. Sunday School Union, 1888.

Pearson, Edward A. *Designs against Charleston: The Trial Record of the Denmark Vesey Slave Conspiracy of 1822.* Chapel Hill: University of North Carolina Press, 1999.

Penn, William. *Fruits of Solitude, in Reflections and Maxims Relating to the Conduct of Human Life.* 9th ed. London: James Phillips, 1778.

Perry, Seth. *Bible Culture and Authority in the Early United States.* Princeton, NJ: Princeton University Press, 2018.

Peterson, Thomas V. *Ham and Japheth in America: The Mythic World of Whites in the Antebellum South.* Metuchen, NJ: American Theological Library Association, 1978.

Pinn, Anthony B. *African American Humanistic Principles: Living and Thinking like the Children of Nimrod.* New York: Palgrave Macmillan, 2004.

Pinn, Anthony B., and Allen Dwight Callahan, eds. *African American Religious Life and the Story of Nimrod.* New York: Palgrave Macmillan, 2008.

Powery, Emerson B., and Rodney S. Sadler Jr. *The Genesis of Liberation: Biblical Interpretation in the Antebellum Narratives of the Enslaved.* Louisville, KY: Westminster John Knox, 2016.

Princeton University. *General Catalogue of Princeton University 1746–1906.* Princeton, NJ: The University, 1908.

Raboteau, Albert. "African Americans, Exodus and American Israel." In *African American Christianity: Essays in History*, edited by Paul E. Johnson, 1–17. Berkeley: University of California Press, 1994.

Raymond, Daniel. *Thoughts on Political Economy: In Two Parts.* Baltimore, MD: Fielding Lucas Jr., 1820.

Reed, Justin Michael. "The Injustice of Noah's Curse and the Presumption of Canaanite Guilt: A New Reading of Genesis 9:18–29." PhD diss., Princeton Theological Seminary, 2020.

Robertson, David. *Denmark Vesey.* New York: Alfred A. Knopf, 1999.

Rucker, Walter C. *The River Flows On: Black Resistance, Culture, and Identity Formation in Early America.* Baton Rouge: Louisiana State University Press, 2006.

Saffin, John. "A Brief and Candid Answer to a Late Printed Sheet, Entitled, The Selling of Joseph." 1701. In *Notes on the History of Slavery in Massachusetts*, edited by George H. Moore, 251–56. New York: D. Appleton and Co., 1866.

Schipper, Jeremy. "The Blessing of Ham: Genesis 9:1 in Early African American Scholarship." *Biblical Interpretation* (forthcoming).

———. "'Misconstruction of the Sacred Page': On Denmark Vesey's Biblical Interpretations." *Journal of Biblical Literature* 138 (2019): 23–38.

———. "'On Such Texts Comment Is Unnecessary': Biblical Interpretation in the Trial of Denmark Vesey." *Journal of the American Academy of Religion* 85 (2017): 1032–49.

———. "Religion, Race and the Wife of Ham." *Journal of Religion* 100 (2020): 386–401.

Schwarz, Philip J. *Gabriel's Conspiracy: A Documentary History.* Charlottesville: University of Virginia Press, 2012.

Sewall, Samuel. *The Selling of Joseph: A Memorial.* Boston: Bartholomew Green and John Allen, 1700.

Shelley, Percy Bysshe. *Queen Mab: A Philosophical Poem; With Notes.* London: Printed by P. B. Shelley, 1813.

Sidbury, James. "Reading, Revelation, and Rebellion: The Textual Communities of Gabriel, Denmark Vesey, and Nat Turner." In *Nat Turner: A Slave Rebellion in History and Memory*, edited by Kenneth S. Greenberg, 119–33. New York: Oxford University Press, 2003.

Sidney, Algernon. *Discourses concerning Government.* 2nd ed. London: J. Darby, 1704.

Simms, William Gilmore. *The History of South Carolina, from Its First European Discovery to Its Erection into a Republic.* Charleston, SC: S. Babcock and Co., 1840.

Smith, Mark M. *Stono: Documenting and Interpreting a Southern Slave Revolt.* Columbia: University of South Carolina Press, 2006.

Smith, Theophus H. *Conjuring Culture: Biblical Formulations of Black America.* New York: Oxford University Press, 1994.

Snay, Michael. *Gospel of Disunion: Religion and Separatism in the Antebellum South.* New York: Cambridge University Press, 1993.

Society of the Cincinnati. *The Original Institution of the General Society of the Cincinnati, as Formed by the Officers of the Army of the United States, at the Conclusion of the Revolutionary War, Which Gave Independence to America.* Charleston, SC: Walker and James, 1849.

Spady, James O'Neil. "Power and Confession: On the Credibility of the Earliest Reports of the Denmark Vesey Slave Conspiracy." *William and Mary Quarterly* 68 (2011): 287–304.

Starobin, Robert S., ed. *Denmark Vesey: The Slave Conspiracy of 1822.* Englewood Cliffs, NJ: Prentice Hall, 1970.

Stout, Harry. *Upon the Altar of the Nation: A Moral History of the Civil War.* New York: Penguin, 2007.

Stowe, Harriett Beecher. *Dred: A Tale of the Great Dismal Swamp.* 2 vols. Boston: Phillips, Sampson and Co., 1856.

Thomas, Rhondda Robinson. *Claiming Exodus: A Cultural History of Afro-Atlantic Identity, 1774–1903.* Waco, TX: Baylor University Press, 2013.

Wade, Richard C. "The Vesey Plot: A Reconsideration." *Journal of Southern History* 30 (1964): 143–61.

Washington, Margaret. "The Meaning of Scripture in Gullah Concepts of Liberation and Group Identity." In *African Americans and the Bible: Sacred Texts and Social Textures,* edited by Vincent L. Wimbush, 321–41. New York: Continuum, 2001.

Whitford, David M. *The Curse of Ham in the Early Modern Era: The Bible and the Justifications for Slavery.* St. Andrews Studies in Reformation History. Burlington, VT: Ashgate, 2009.

Williams, George Washington. *History of the Negro Race in America from 1619 to 1881: Negroes as Slaves, as Soldiers, and as Citizens; Together with a Preliminary Consideration of the Unity of the Human Family, an Historical Sketch of Africa, and an Account of the Negro Governments of Sierra Leone and Liberia.* 2 vols. New York: G. P. Putnam's Sons, 1882.

Yale University. *Catalogue of the Officers and Graduates of Yale University in New Haven, Connecticut. 1701–1893.* New Haven, CT: Tuttle, Morehouse and Taylor, 1892.

Young, Jeffrey Robert. *Domesticating Slavery: The Master Class in Georgia and South Carolina, 1670–1837.* Chapel Hill: University of North Carolina Press, 1999.

IMAGE CREDITS

Figure 1. Map of Charleston. Wikimedia Commons: https://commons.wikimedia
.org/wiki/File:1849_map_of_Charleston,_South_Carolina.jpeg.

Figure 2. Emanuel African Methodist Episcopal Church (present day). Photo by
jalexartis Photography. Licensed under CC BY 2.0. https://www.flickr.com
/photos/fayncbikerjaa/18802468310/in/album-72157652502690263.

Figure 3. Execution list in Kennedy and Parker's *Official Report*. Library of
Congress Rare Book and Special Collections Division, KF223.V4
V47 1822.

Figure 4. Title page of Kennedy and Parker's *Official Report*. Library of Congress
Rare Book and Special Collections Division, KF223.V4 V47 1822.

Figure 5. The Circular Congregational Church. Library of Congress Prints
and Photographs Division, LOT 4163, no. 9.

Figure 6. Old Charleston jail. Photo by Michael Rivera on Wikimedia
Commons. Licensed under CC A-S 4.0. Wikimedia Commons:
https://commons.wikimedia.org/wiki/File:Old_Charleston_Jail
_south_face_entrance.jpg.

Figure 7. Denmark Vesey monument in Hampton Park, Charleston. Photo by
ProfReader on Wikimedia Commons. Licensed under CC A-S 4.0.
Wikimedia Commons: https://commons.wikimedia.org/wiki
/File:Vesey.jpg.

INDEX

Note: Page numbers in *italics* indicate illustrations.

Printed in the USA
CPSIA information can be obtained
at www.ICGtesting.com
JSHW031922230224
57955JS00001B/9